The Creek Captives

With an eye made quiet by the power
Of harmony . . .
We see into the life of things.
. . . Therefore am I still
A lover of the meadows and the woods
And mountains, and of all that we behold
From this green earth . . .

>	Wordsworth
>	"Lines from Tintern Abbey"

THE CREEK CAPTIVES

Helen Blackshear
with an introduction by Dr. Ed Bridges

NewSouth Books
Montgomery | Louisville

NewSouth Books
P.O. Box 1588
Montgomery, AL 36102

Copyright © 2007 by Helen Blackshear
All rights reserved under International and Pan-American Copyright Conventions.
Published in the United States by Junebug Books, a division of NewSouth, Inc.,
Montgomery, Alabama.

ISBN-13: 978-1-60306-021-9

ISBN-10: 1-60306-021-9

Design by Randall Williams
Printed in the United States of America

First Edition 1975
Second Edition, with three new stories, 1990
Third Edition 2001
Fourth Edition 2007

Contents

Foreword 7
Preface to Third Edition 9
The Creek Captives 15
Sam Dale and the Long-tailed Blue 67
The Dance of Death 73
The Whipping 82
Half-Breed Billy 97
The Stagecoach Ride 117
Ride a White Horse 129
Bibliography 144

Foreword

Dr. Ed Bridges, Director
Alabama Department of Archives and History

WHEN WE THINK of early Alabama history, mental pictures of antebellum plantations tend to crowd out everything else. We forget that the years of grand plantation homes were relatively brief. Most were built less than a generation before the Civil War. The percentage of early Alabamians who lived in these homes was very small.

The reality of early Alabama history was more complex, and more interesting. When the first Spanish troups led by Hernando de Soto crossed Alabama in 1540, they found a complex and impressive Indian civilization we call Mississippian. The diseases and destruction of the Europeans brought the end of the Mississippian culture. The new Indian powers that emerged through the 1600s and 1700s were the Creeks, the Cherokees, the Choctaws, and the Chickasaws. From the last half of the 1600s through the first half of the 1800s, these Indian nations struggled to take advantage of what the European powers offered them but to avoid being dominated by the Europeans.

Helen Blackshear's stories begin in the latter years of these struggles. The French have already left Alabama, but their memories and even some of their children — born of Indian wives — remain.

English and Scottish traders and their children, also born to Indian wives, live among the Indians. So do a substantial number of Africans, some of whom are slaves and some of whom are free. The Spanish, still in control of Florida, are a source the Indians turn to for both supplies and military support.

By the late 1700s the main threat to the Indians has clearly become the newly created United States. As their crops and agricultural practices wear out their old land, American settlers look with increasing longing at the rich, fertile land of Alabama. Mrs. Blackshear's stories show the remarkable changes in this land, from this time of initial American settlement through the end of the Civil War. Within the span of one full lifetime, we see Alabama change from a land of Indians defending themselves against outside invaders to a land of Confederates, also reeling under the attack of invading forces.

In this too-much overlooked period of Alabama history, Mrs. Blackshear has found a treasure-trove of great stories. Using the written recollections of people who lived through this time, she has put together her stories based on actual people and events. Through these stories we see the last proud stands of Alabama Indians and the daring struggles of the new immigrants. This is reality of high drama — of brutal conflict, meanness, and tragedy, and of heroic effort, kindness, and nobility of character. These stories need to be told, retold, and understood. For such a fine job of telling them again, we are in Mrs. Blackshear's debt.

Preface to Third Edition

ALABAMA HAS BEEN fortunate in her historians. Even during the time of DeSoto and Bienville there were men who wrote down and preserved their observations of these events. We have been fortunate, too, in the quality of our Indian agents. In Colonial times there was Thomas Woodward, who became the first white friend of the Creeks and who won them to the side of the English. Later there was Colonel John Tate, the last Indian agent sent by the British, who lived among the Creeks near old Fort Toulouse. Before his death in a frontier battle in 1780, he married a Creek princess and through his son David Tate became the ancestor of many important Alabama families.

After the Revolutionary War, Colonel Marinus Willett was sent by President George Washington in 1790 to seek peace with Chief Alexander McGillivray of the Creeks. His letters describe his success and the journey of the Creek chiefs to New York. President Washington's appointment of Benjamin Hawkins as agent to the Creeks in 1796 resulted in twenty years of peaceful development. On the Tombigbee River, the highly respected Colonel George Gaines won the admiration and friendship of the Choctaws.

Then there were the travelers — the French Colonel LeClerc Milfort, who married McGillivray's sister and wrote a memoir of his years among her people. The naturalist Bartram visited and described the Creeks, as did John Pope on his tour in 1792. The historian A. J. Pickett often visited the Creek villages and listened to their stories. There have been others — Peter Brannon, Thomas M. Owen, and Marie Bankhead Owen, and many more recent scholars who have mined the rich material of Alabama's past. It is to them and to all fellow lovers of history that I dedicate these Alabama stories.

My grateful thanks to the late Milo Howard, Director of the Alabama Archives and History Department, for advice on sources; to Craig Ray, archeologist with the Alabama Historical Commission, who checked for historical accuracy; and especially to my late husband for his enduring patience and encouragement.

The Creek Captives was published in 1975 in a small limited edition which quickly sold out. It contained only four stories, although the events in these stories spanned almost a century, from 1790 to 1864.

In 1990, Randall Williams published an expanded edition of the book at his then-new publishing venture, Black Belt Press. To round out the picture of Alabama's pioneer days, the new edition contained two new stories concerning Sam Dale, one of the most colorful characters of Alabama's early days, and a third story about the state's last Indian uprising, which took place on the then-frontier between Montgomery and Columbus, Georgia.

That second edition of the book stayed in print through most of the 1990s. The present book, with a new cover and interior design, is the third edition.

In the original stories, as in the more recent additions, my hope has been that presenting true events in which young people were involved would stir the interest of today's young readers in Alabama's fascinating pioneer history.

HELEN F. BLACKSHEAR

The Creek Captives

The Creek Captives

AT FIRST NED felt only the throbbing pain in his head. He tried opening his eyes, but the glare hurt them and the ground seemed to sway dizzily upward to meet him so he shut them again hastily. When he tried to move his arms, he became aware that they were bound to his body with rawhide thongs and that he had been slung face downward across a jogging pack horse. The sun was beating straight down and sweat was dripping from his tangled yellow hair, so it must be around noon. He must have been unconscious for hours! Something was nagging at him, something he had to remember yet was afraid to, something horrible . . .

Suddenly a picture from the early morning flashed across his mind, as clearly as though he were outside the log cabin watching another boy and his father as the painted Indians careened through the yard on their ponies, making their strange gobbling sounds. Ned saw his father straighten up from the cabin window with a triumphant cry, "Got one of 'em, by golly!" Then there was a surprised look on Pa's face as he fell forward with blood pouring out of his mouth.

Ned recalled hearing a muffled gasp from the loft where Ma and little Becky were hiding, and how he was silently begging them to stay quiet so he could protect them. The last thing he could remember was trying to hold Pa's long rifle steady on a capering

Indian with a plumed head dress and a fancy ruffled shirt that hung open above his breechclout.

The gun had been almost too heavy for Ned's slender hands, and he wished he were not so weak from swamp fever. Then he had caught the unmistakable rancid smell of bear oil and he knew that one of the Indians had crept up behind him. That was when the blow came that had knocked him out. He winced again, remembering, and nausea rose to his throat. Then mercifully he drifted back into unconsciousness.

It was night time when he again opened his eyes. He could tell by the sounds of the tree frogs and a distant whippoorwill. The air felt cool and damp and he could hear a creek off somewhere running over rocks. His bands were untied now. He stretched them gratefully and felt the cane matting under him. Smoke drifted toward the rafters of the lodge and he could dimly make out some objects hanging there in the fire shadows, heads of animals, it looked like, or were they masks? There was a shriveled old Indian asleep across the room. He had skeleton ribs and was naked except for his breechclout.

A dim, bundled-up figure stirred beside him. He caught a brief glitter of eyes in the firelight and looked into the wrinkled face of an old Indian woman. When she saw that he was awake she held a wooden bowl to his lips. His head still hurt when he raised it, but he was surprised to find that he was hungry and the stew tasted good. Then the old crone brought him a gourd with a hot drink in it and gabbled something at him in their strange language. The stuff was bitter and he spat it out, but she put her claw-like hand on his forehead and pointed to the gourd. Ned figured it must be medicine for his head and made himself take a big swallow. Then he lay back exhausted and drifted into sleep.

When he woke again it was morning and he was alone in the lodge. His homespun breeches and shirt were drenched in sweat, and his head felt light and clear as if his fever had broken. Maybe the old woman's brew had done that, he thought, and wondered if she would come to feed him again. Then he felt angry at himself that he could think of food when he didn't know yet what awful things might have happened to Ma and Becky.

Ma was quick and strong, and if she was alive she could probably outsmart any old Indian, he thought, but Becky was only ten, three years younger than himself. A memory of Becky's freckled face and dark braids swam before him, and he hated himself for all the times he had pushed her away when she wanted to tag after him and ask a million questions. He never saw such a girl for wanting to know everything. Then he thought he must be dreaming because he heard Becky's voice on the other side of the plastered log wall near his head.

"Ned! Ned, are you in there? Please answer me. Please!"

"Becky!" he yelled, suddenly finding his voice. "Thank the Lord! Is Ma all right? How'd you find me?"

"I saw them take you in there, but I couldn't slip off till now. The squaws are working Ma like a slave but they just put me with the other kids," Becky answered softly. "Listen, somebody's coming so I'll skeedaddle, but I'll be back tonight."

In his excitement Ned had tried to get up, but he was still weak as a kitten. He fell back exhausted just as the old squaw came in with a bowl of corn meal mush. He'd have to get his strength back before he could do anything to help Ma and Becky. As he lay there watching the Indian woman putter around the fire, he let his mind go back to that day at the tavern when the old trapper had warned Pa against crossing the Oconee River. Ever since then Ned had had a scary feeling, especially when he and Pa went into the deep woods after game. It seemed like there were eyes out there watching him from the shadows, and sometimes he had to stop himself from turning to stare back over his shoulder.

That old trader had known what he was talking about, Ned thought, though at the time his Pa had said the old fellow was just trying to scare them off. "That old man has got a good thing going, tradin' with the Creek Indians, an' he don't want newcomers poachin' on his territory," Joseph Brown had claimed when he and Ned had gone back to join Ma and Becky in the wagon.

"He says the Creeks have been patrolin' the boundary since the survey last year an' keepin' settlers out. But Smithers an' his boys have been trappin' over there 'cross the Oconee since Fall, an' he's brought in the finest pelts I ever saw. He's talkin' now about clearin' ground for spring crops — says that bottom land is twice as rich as what he had back in Carolina."

Ma had been doubtful of the new move from the beginning. Ned had begun to realize that Jane Brown, with her square chin and calm grey eyes, was the practical one of his parents. She thought ahead and found a way to make things work. Ma's father back in North Carolina was a well-off farmer who hadn't liked his daughter's marrying a young man without a penny to his name, even though he was the handsomest one around and one of Swamp Fox Marion's heroes to boot. Ned could see how his Ma had fallen in love with Pa's songs and stories. Pa had kept them spellbound many a night telling about how Marion's men had tricked the Tories during the war and how they'd lived hidden in the woods like Indians. Pa had been a fine woodsman himself and had built them a right snug cabin.

Ned rolled over on the cane mat and buried his head in his arms as he remembered Pa the way he'd last seen him, happy over killing the Indian and reckless as always, forgetting to keep behind the window sill. Now Pa was dead and Ma was a slave. Ned's clinched fists beat on the mat as he cursed his own weakness.

A vague plan began to form in his mind. He would rest all day. Then tonight when the old squaw was asleep, he would practice flexing his muscles and make another try at crawling off the mat. The thought eased his worry a little, and again he fell asleep.

It was late afternoon when Ned woke and he felt much stronger and ravenously hungry. He called to the old squaw and pointed to his mouth, making gestures as though he were eating. She gabbled at him and brought him mush with pieces of meat in it. "Sofia," she told him, pointing to the bowl.

Ned pronounced it after her, "So-fi-a." It was his first Indian word. Then he remembered his plan and fell back as though he were too weak to raise his head. Behind his closed eyes, though, his thoughts were racing. Outside the lodge now he could hear people gathering for a celebration — voices shouting back and forth, the wailing of reed pipes, loud laughter that sounded like the Indians had been drinking tafia, the cheap rum that so many of them had a weakness for.

When it grew dark outside, Ned pretended to be asleep while the old woman stood above him. From under his eyelids he watched her slip outside and return a short time later reeking of tafia. Soon she was snoring as she huddled over the small central fire. Ned peered into the shadows behind her but there was no sign of the old man.

When he tried to stand up, his knees promptly buckled, and only his outspread hands saved him from hitting the dirt floor with his face. Then he tried crawling, inching himself forward on his elbows with frequent stops to rest. Finally he reached the doorway and pushed aside the deerskin curtain with his hand.

Ned would never forget that savage fire-lit scene with its backdrop of hovering forest. Four big lodges faced a lighted square and he could see rows of Indians seated on raised benches along the open porches, all watching the dancing. Over the throbbing of the drums he could still hear the sound of running water and decided the creek must be directly behind this lodge. The figures capering around the fire were too far off for him to distinguish clearly. He must get closer, but he could never make it that far.

With a sigh of relief he heard Becky's piercing whisper, "S - s - st! Ned! I've been waiting here forever. Can you crawl this far?"

Her voice came from around the corner of the lodge, and Ned slowly pulled himself along the plastered log wall to find the small girl huddled behind a big rhododendron bush. "Hi, Sis! Sorry I'm so bushed," he gasped weakly.

"I crept along under the creek bank," she whispered. "I couldn't get near Ma — they watch her too close — but it wasn't hard for me to slip off while they were celebrating."

"What's all the celebratin' about?" asked Ned.

"Oh, Ned," moaned Becky, and to his dismay she began to sob. When he got her calmed down she went on, "They've got Pa's scalp and all the Smithers' scalps up on a big pole with snakes carved on it. One of the Indian girls has been tryin' to talk to me an' I figured out from her that this tribe is called the Autossees — that means Snakes — and they're just like 'em, sneakin' up on our cabin and killin' Pa, Oh, I hate 'em!"

Ned tried to control his own surge of hatred for these bloodthirsty savages and broke in quickly before Becky could start cryin again, "Listen, Becky, you've got to stay cool. You're the only hope we've got for keepin' in contact. I'm no use till I get stronger. Keep your eyes and ears open an' come back here tomorrow night. Daytime's too dangerous. Scratch on the wall here outside my bed an' I'll knock twice if it's safe to talk. Now maybe you better help me back to my door before that squaw wakes up."

That night's visit established a pattern for the week that followed. It was easier for them to talk after Ned managed to chip a small hole in the plaster close to his ear. He figured the old woman was half deaf anyway, and she left him pretty much alone except for the twice a day feedings and the bitter medicine. Once, to his horror, she had stripped off his filthy clothes and left him naked and trembling all morning. At noon, though, when she brought them back clean and smelling of sun, Ned smiled at her for the first time. Now he felt almost human again.

He had kept up his secret exercises and wondered how long he could continue the pretense of weakness. He gritted his teeth with impatience every time he thought of Ma being poked and scratched with gar teeth to make her work faster and tied up at night to her lodge pole. Then suddenly, on the tenth day after their capture, everything changed.

Becky hurried to the wall so excited she could hardly talk. That afternoon, she told Ned, a big bunch of pack horses and cattle had been driven into the Autossee town by two Indian boys and two Negro slaves. They were led by a tall, white-haired Negro man. Becky had gotten the idea from her Indian girl friend that they had brought the stock to exchange for the captives.

Becky giggled. "She says you and me are worth six horses and three cows apiece, but Ma's worth twice as much 'cause she can do more work."

After Becky left, Ned could hardly get to sleep for wondering who had ransomed them and what would happen next. At daybreak next morning the two slaves came to Ned's lodge leading a horse. To his surprise they spoke English. "Can you ride or do you want us to tie you on?" one of them asked.

"I reckon I can hang on all right," grinned Ned. "I been playin' sick lately till I could figger out how to get loose. Where are you takin' us?"

He learned from the slaves that their master was Colonel Alexander McGillivray, whom they described as the biggest chief in the Creek Nation, and that the white-haired Paro was his top man. "Ev'ybody in de Nation know dat Paro speak fo' de mastah," continued the slave named Lucas. "Cunnel McGillivray get so mad he fit to be tied when he learn 'bout any of his peoples sheddin' white folks' blood an' stealin' dey fam'lies. Dis de second time dis yeah dat he sen' Paro and us to ransom folks and git 'em back to dey peoples."

Then the slaves led Ned's horse to a huddled group on the outskirts of the sleeping village. Becky and Ma greeted him with glad cries, but old Paro gestured for silence as they moved out into a dim wooded trail shrouded in morning mist.

Ned was shocked at his mother's appearance. Her face and arms were scratched and bruised, her dress ragged and dirty, and her hair a tangled mass. He had never before seen her when she was not neatly dressed and her brown hair clean and soft. But Ma's eyes lighted up when she saw him, and he was soon reassured by the matter of fact tone of her voice. "What a kind man your master must be to do so much for strangers!" she said to Paro. "We are truly grateful. And if I can just have ten minutes to wash in the first stream we come to, if that is possible . . ."

"Indeed you can, madam, an' Colonel McGillivray's sister, Miss Sehoy, she'll be glad to welcome you to her home. My massah would invite you to his own place, but his missus been feelin' po'ly and Mastah's laid up wid de gout. He sent young Master David, Miss Sehoy's boy, to he'p guide you to his home." The old Negro gestured toward the slim boy on a big black horse whom Ned had taken at first glance to be an Indian.

Now, as the day brightened, he could see that the boy called David had a mane of light brown hair and very blue eyes in a suntanned face. Ned had been misled by the quilled head dress and the buckskin tunic and calf-high beaded moccasins. David had a quiver of arrows slung across his shoulders, too, and carried a long bow, something Ned had been longing for. Pa's rifle had been too heavy and noisy for him, but with a bow and arrow he could creep up close to small game without alarming it. He spurred his horse forward and said tentatively, "I've been admiring that bow. Did you make it?"

David smiled. He had a nice smile, his teeth showing very white in his tanned face. "Well, I helped make it," he said, "but Paro showed me how. Paro can make 'most anything with wood or cane — whistles, flutes, even dolls for my sisters. Maybe later on we can ask him to show you how to make a bow."

"Say, that would be great!" exclaimed Ned. For the first time since their capture, he felt the stirring of excitement and curiosity about their destination. The air was so fresh here after the smoky dimness of the Indian lodge, and long rays of sunlight slanted across the trail. Only their voices and the muffled sound of the horses' hooves on pine straw disturbed the morning stillness. He would have liked to talk longer with his new acquaintance, but David and Chocco, the Indian boy, rode ahead or parallel to the party to protect them from ambush.

After an hour of riding they came to a small clear stream where Paro called a halt for rest. Becky and her mother hurried along the bank, and soon Ned heard them laughing and splashing as they bathed. He slid gratefully from his horse but had to cling to the mane for a few moments before his legs stopped trembling from weakness. He mumbled a shamed apology to David, who rode in from the woods just in time to help him to a seat on the mossy bank.

"It's not just being knocked out by those Indians. I was sick a long time before that. Ma says I was out of my head a while. I was jus' gettin' over it when those Autossees burned our cabin an' killed Pa." There was still a trace of anger in Ned's voice as he added, "I thought at first you were an Indian, the way you're dressed."

"But I do have Indian blood," answered David proudly. "My mother's mother was Princess Sehoy of the Wind tribe, and Mother's named for her. That's the tribe most of our greatest chiefs have been chosen from. Don't judge all Indians by those Autossees. They are a mean bunch who hate all whites. They've had lots of run-ins with the Georgians."

"You look more white than Indian, though. Was your father white?" asked Ned.

"Yes, he was an English officer, Colonel John Tate. He was killed in battle when I was a baby, so I never knew him. My mother's father was Lachlan McGillivray. He was a Scotch trader who lived among the Creeks until the Americans ran him out after the war. They took over all his Georgia land because he was a Tory. Then my stepfather, Charles Weatherford, is English, too. You'll meet him when we get home."

Home . . .the word brought a lump into Ned's throat. He said in a strangled voice, "My Pa fought the English with Swamp Fox Marion. They chased those old Tories all across Carolina!" He glared at David Tate.

For a startled moment David glared back. Then suddenly he laughed. "Say, that war's been over for a few years now, unless you want to start another one with me! I 'spect I could take you on right now."

Ned glanced down ruefully at his thin legs and pale arms. "You sure could, at that. Ah well, it's not our fight, I guess, though I was brought up to think all Tories were bad men. What say we call a truce — at least until I get stronger!" He grinned and stuck out his hand. David grasped it with a smile, then he raised his hand in parting as he rode off to take up his flanking position.

At noon they stopped at a wide creek whose banks were shadowed by moss-hung trees. Ned noticed Lucas and his fellow slave Jonas looking around fearfully and whispering together. The dense shade and damp air did give a sinister feel to this place, Ned thought, and he was not surprised when the little party drew closer together as Paro distributed jerky and biscuits from the pack saddles. "Ah be glad when us gits across dis here Murder Creek," muttered Lucas. "Ah don' like dis place at all!"

"What does he mean, Paro?" Becky asked. "Why is it called Murder Creek?" She had been riding beside the old Negro all the way and bombarding him with questions, but Paro didn't seem to mind.

He answered her gently in his well-modulated voice, "It's a long fearsome story, little Missy, not fit for yo' ears. Best wait till we get safe across this here creek."

Then Paro directed the slaves and Chocco, the silent Indian boy who followed David like a shadow, in the building of a raft. From the dense thicket along the bank they cut large canes ten feet long and tied them into bundles three feet in circumference. Across these others were laid and tied in place with long grapevines. Then other vines were used to guide the raft across.

Ned was too tired to protest Paro's insistence that he ride on the raft with Ma and Becky, but he envied David and the other boys as they swam their horses through the swift current. When all were safely on the opposite bank, Becky again begged Paro for his story.

For answer the old man pointed his long arm toward a giant tree with a horizontal branch that protruded over the small clearing. "Yonder tree was where it all happened," he said slowly, his eyes looking sad and far away. 'They hung Colonel Kirkland and two men to that very limb!'

"Lord, dat wuz an awful night," moaned Lucas. "I nebba tho't I'd live to tell uv it!"

"But who murdered them, and why did they do it?" pleaded Becky. "Go on, Paro!"

Paro resumed his talk. "Why, honey, Colonel Kirkland was a rich traveler, with fine clothes and a heap of gold in his pouch to trade with in Pensacola. The master sent me and two helpers

— Lucas here was one of 'em — to guide him on the trail. Right here on this bank was where we camped for the night." He looked again at the big tree.

"But who were the murderers?" Becky persisted. "Were they bad Indians like those that killed Pa?"

Ned saw his mother's face grow sad at the memory and wished Becky were not so outspoken. But he, too, was eager to hear the grim story.

"Ain't no race of people got all the bad men, honey," answered Paro softly. "Only one of these men was an Indian, a Hillabee named Istillicha — that means Man-slayer. He'd been run off by his own people. The next man was a sorry black man who used to belong to a half-breed trader named Sullivan, a mean old coot who used to train this black man to steal and kill for him. Well, one day he ran off and teamed up with that Hillabee Indian. But the worst one of the three was a white man. They called him the Cat, after the Cat tribe of Indians he took up with, and that was the only name anybody ever knew. This murder had his mark all over it — quick and silent like a panther."

"What did they do?" whispered Ned eagerly, and David's blue eyes were shining with interest, though he had heard the story before.

"They crept upon them in the dark of night whilst they were sleeping and cut their throats," said Paro grimly. "Then they hung 'em to that limb by their feet like you'd hang a turkey."

Ned shuddered, remembering how Pa had hung their fresh-killed Christmas turkey up to drip before Ma scalded it to remove the feathers. "Why didn't they kill you and Lucas, too?" he asked.

"Just plain luck, boy," said Paro fervently while Lucas echoed a heartfelt "Amen." "You see, I generally put up a little brush shelter to sleep in, to keep off the night wind from my rheumatism." He chuckled. "Well, I offered to make one for the gentlemen, but they said they'd just as soon sleep in the open as it was a mild night."

"Me and the boys went on to sleep then, leavin' them talkin' by the fire. Next thing I knew I was woke up by a kind of gaspin' sound like somebody started to scream and it was shut off. I woke the boys up real careful like, but by the time we peeked out through the bushes we saw it was all over. There wasn't a thing we could do! The murderers was already pullin' those three bodies up onto that limb!"

Ned shuddered, and Becky let out her held breath with a gasp. "Gosh! How did you ever get away without them catching you?"

"We just froze," said Paro solemnly, "till they got so excited over finding all that gold. Then we crept down to the creek so we couldn't be trailed and finally made it home on foot."

"Were the murderers ever caught?" asked Ned, involuntarily looking over his shoulder into the shadowy woods.

"My master sent out warriors to comb the Nation, but they never found a trace of the Indian or the black man. But General Milford — he's the master's French brother-in-law — he came onto the track of the Cat one day and finally they got him cornered. They hung him to that selfsame limb!" He gestured toward it with his head. "And that's how come they call this Murder Creek!"

They were all glad to leave this gloomy spot behind them, and the spirits of the party lightened as the trail began to follow a high ridge where the air was dear and golden. Ned lost track of the creeks and rivers they crossed. He soon understood how the Creek Indians had gotten their name, for the villages they passed through were invariably beside running water. Often they caught the flash of a copper-colored boy arching into a stream, for these Indian children were as graceful as fish in the water. It was a lush green land, much richer looking than the red clay Georgia hills he remembered from early childhood.

The lodges around the squares of the Creek villages were built of plastered logs like the Autossee one where Ned had been kept prisoner. The Indians he saw were clean and healthy-looking people. Paro told Ned that most of their ceremonies such as the Green Corn Dance, or Boos-ke-tau, as they called it, included swimming in the creeks after purging themselves of impurities with their "black drink," a sort of medicine made from casina leaves. Ned wondered if that was what the old squaw had given him to drink.

Once they passed through a town of the Alabama tribe. Paro told him that these people had been conquered long ago by the Creeks and that they did not speak Muskogee, the Creek mother tongue, but used what he called scornfully a "stinkard lingo." Becky said she liked the sound of the Muskogee language and wanted to learn more words. She would point to trees and flowers along the trail and ask Paro their Indian names. Ned found that the sounds did not seem so strange to him now. In fact, some of them were almost like music.

In all these towns Ned noticed that Paro was welcomed and treated with respect, but Paro modestly claimed that this was not a tribute to him personally but to Chief Alexander McGillivray. "They make me welcome because they love my master," he said proudly. "They know he's the only chief they ever had that can keep peace and hold all the Creek tribes together. When one bunch misbehaves, like those Autossees that took you prisoner, he'll punish them by not lettin' traders visit their villages. My master don't like fightin' any of 'em less he has to, but they soon come to terms if he shuts off their supply of rum and trinkets!"

Ned was becoming increasingly curious about this master of Paro's whom everyone seemed to admire. So far the only chief he had seen close up had been a malicious-looking old Coosawda who had peering eyes and a big nose under his gaudy plumed head dress and a naked chest hung with medals and ornaments. When the tired travelers finally reached Hickory Ground, however, after three more long days on the trail, Ned found Chief Alexander McGillivray and his house very different from what he had expected.

It was late afternoon when they rode into a typical Creek village built on a bluff overlooking the junction of the Coosa and Tallapoosa rivers. Ned had thought they would be taken to the chief's lodge at the west end of the square, but they rode right on through the town. "My master lives on his own plantation," Paro explained. "It's 'bout three miles further on down the road. Here come some of his people now to meet us."

Ned heard shouts of welcome and slaves approached them, and just before sundown they came to the porch of a comfortable looking two-story house set back in a sheltering grove of trees. As soon as the weary travelers had rested and refreshed themselves, they were told that Colonel McGillivray was waiting in the library to receive them. David Tate said good-bye to them in the wide entrance hall of the manor house after running to the library door for a few words of greeting to his uncle. "I want to hurry on home to tell my mother you'll be coming to our house tomorrow," he told Ned. "She'll be pleased. She loves company, 'specially when it's another woman." He smiled at Jane Brown, who clasped his hand and smiled gratefully in return.

"Thank your mother for us and tell her we'll try not to be a bother to her. It's a good feeling to be made welcome after what we've been through!"

Then a short buxom Indian housekeeper with dark braids and dressed in a beaded tunic was ushering them into the book-lined library where a pale, scholarly looking man lay on a couch, his swollen, bandaged foot propped up on a pillow. Ned felt awkward and out of place in the comfortably furnished room with its thick rugs and beautiful ornaments. It was like a room he had once seen through a lighted window of a rich plantation house they had passed back in Georgia. The only thing that looked Indian was the gayly colored wall hangings on each side of the cheerful fireplace.

Alexander McGillivray did not look a thing like Ned's idea of an Indian chief either. He was dressed like any rich Southern planter in an embroidered velvet lounging jacket and broadcloth trousers, his chestnut-brown hair tied back neatly from his high forehead, and the slim, tapering fingers stretched out to greet them were those of a man not used to manual labor. It was his piercing dark eyes and strong voice, thought Ned, that showed that this was a man of power, in spite of his illness. You sensed it the minute you came into the room, and Ned began to understand why Paro and David spoke of him with respect and affection.

Colonel McGillivray was apologizing for not rising to greet Mrs. Brown, gesturing wryly toward his bandaged foot. Then he was asking about their journey and promising to do his best to make amends for the cruel treatment of the Autossees, who had disobeyed his express orders. "The Creek Nation, as you know, stretches all the way from the Cumberland Valley to Mobile, and to the Oconee River in Georgia. We try hard to keep the peace. There are many others like my faithful Paro who hurry to put down violence whenever it breaks out, but many of my people are like willful children. When they are provoked they act in haste and bring danger to the peace of all of us." He shook his head sadly.

Ned was proud of Ma. She acted like she was used to being in fine rooms like this one and she answered Colonel McGillivray's questions in her soft voice without any hesitation. Ned listened to her now as she replied to the chief's expression of regret for Pa's death.

"I can't pretend I'm not sad and bitter over it, sir," she said with a little break in her voice. "He was warned not to cross the boundary, and I was always against it. But he was sore tempted by the tales of the rich lands and fine pelts. Now that I've seen for myself what a bountiful rich land it is, it's hard to fault him, sir."

Ma hung her head, and Colonel McGillivray's stern expression softened. "It's true we have allowed a few white traders and ranchers to settle among us," he admitted, "but they have been ones who were willing to accept our ways and choose their wives from among our people. I'm sorry to say that some of them, like Savannah Jack up on the Tallapoosa River, are horse thieves and worse, the very scum of the colonies. But even these men, bad as they are, make a sort of protection from the hordes of settlers who would overrun us once we let down the bars. Our first thought, Madam, must always be the preservation of our Creek Nation!" The chief's eyes shone as he said this, and Ned could see why his people looked up to him with such reverence.

Then Ned found his mind wandering, and he grew drowsy from the warmth of the fire. In spite of his efforts to stay awake, his head began to nod. As from a distance he heard the chief's melodious voice saying, "Forgive me! Paro told me your son had been very ill. Let us make you more comfortable for tonight, and tomorrow you will meet my Sister Sehoy."

The voices faded, and Ned found himself being led, half-asleep, into a cool, high-ceilinged bedroom where he kicked off his tattered boots and crawled thankfully under the mosquito netting without removing his clothes. "Gosh! A real featherbed!" was his last thought as he sank into sleep again.

Next morning as he breakfasted with his family, Ned got a clearer idea of Paro's importance from Vicey, the fat Indian housekeeper, as she bustled around their table in the huge kitchen of Hickory Ground plantation. "Paro is boss of all people in the kitchen, smokehouse, all those storehouses." She pointed a plump finger toward the open doorway through which they could see many log sheds and outbuildings. Ned recognized Paro's grizzled head towering above the clusters of men as he moved among them to direct the work of the day.

After breakfast Vicey proudly showed Ma and Becky her well-stocked pantries, where Becky had to ask about the contents of each container. There were huge pots of bear oil, some of them seasoned with herbs and spices ready for use in cooking. Ma was fascinated by the row of big stone crocks that contained great coils of sausages in bear oil, meats pickled in vinegar or packed in salt, wild honey, many kinds of preserves, even cabbage made into something Vicey called sauerkraut. Ned was more interested in the smoked meat that was hung from the rafters by tough strands of yucca palm leaf. He was trying to identify the different varieties of meat when Paro came to the doorway.

"I don' mean to rush you folks, Miz Brown, ma'am, but I know Miz Sehoy an' her little girls are anxious to see you."

"Oh, Paro, why didn't you tell me there were girls?" Becky squealed. "Are they my age? Oh, let's hurry!" Her braids flopped as she jumped up and down in excitement.

Paro looked at Becky judiciously. "Well, I 'spect Missy Rosa's 'bout your age and Missy 'Lizabeth's some younger. Then there's the two little fellers in the nursery. But I'm forgettin'. The mistress asked me to bring you all upstairs to see her before you leave. She's a little better this mornin'."

"I'll be glad to have a chance to thank her." Jane Brown looked down despairingly at her ragged dress, "but I'm sorry I look such a fright."

"Now don't you worry none, ma'am," insisted Paro. "If I know the mistress, she'll already have it in mind how to help you."

This proved to be the case. When they came into the large, airy bedroom where the sick woman lay propped against her pillows on a chaise lounge, Mrs. McGillivray's first thought was about clothes for Ma and Becky. The Creek chief's wife was a pretty woman in spite of her paleness. She was dressed in a green silk robe and wore her dark braids coiled high on her head and adorned with bands of silver. She exclaimed in horror over the bruises and scratches on Jane Brown's arms. "What brutes those Autossees were to treat you so cruelly! And you are so pretty, too, my dear. You must let me give you something to wear. I believe we are about the same size."

She then beckoned to the Indian maid, directing her to take Ned and Becky to the children's schoolroom while she and their mother looked for a suitable dress. "I'm sorry my little Cecie's and Sophy's things would be too small for your Becky, but one of Sehoy's girls is the right size."

It was actually more like a nursery than a schoolroom, Ned thought as they were shown into a long, sunny room where a small boy sat reading while his two sisters played with their dolls in a corner.

"Mister Alex, here's Ned and Becky Brown come to visit you," said the maid as she ushered them into the door and hurried off to help her mistress.

Little Alex greeted them with a happy smile. Becky immediately sat down with the little girls to examine their dolls while Ned walked over to look at Alex's book which had pictures of birds and animals. Though the boy was thin and pale like his mother, his shining dark eyes reminded Ned of Colonel McGillivray. He had a serious, grown-up manner and was full of questions about Ned's journey. "Tell me what it's like in Georgia and North Carolina," he demanded. "Some day I want to go all the way to the other side of the forest. My father says I'm to go to school in Scotland when I'm older."

Ned tried to describe his grandfather's farm home in Guildford Courthouse, North Carolina, and the large coastal cities he had seen as a child. It surprised him to realize how unreal and far away that world seemed to him now. When Alex asked him if he wanted to go back to live in North Carolina, Ned had to stop and think before he could give an honest answer. "Yes, and no," he said finally. "I mean, Ma's set on me getting schooling and all that, and then I'd always planned on being a soldier when I grow up, like Pa was in the Revolution."

Ned still felt a pang of sadness when he thought of Pa's death, but he resolutely put it behind him. "Now that I'm here," he went on thoughtfully, "I want to stay a while and learn more about your people. I sort of like it here. It's not the way I thought it would be at all."

Mrs. Weatherford's plantation was about two miles upriver. Its big house was not as richly furnished or as smoothly run as her brother's, but Ned thought it was a nicer house to live in. It didn't have that hushed feeling of a home where people are sick. The children ran in and out hollering and playing, with dogs running after them. David's mother was a plump, laughing woman who loved to talk, especially about people and clothes. As soon as Ma caught sight of the hand loom with the bright-colored pattern on it, they had started right in talking about weaving and spinning and what styles people were wearing back in Savannah and Charleston, though Ma said her ideas would be way out of date.

Becky had hit it off real well with David's sisters, too. The oldest, Rosie, had a round freckled face and a funny giggle, and little Elizabeth was skinny but looked lively. The younger boys, Jack and Wash, were at the pesky age when they gobbled their food and teased their sisters. It was the kind of house where you felt right at home as soon as you walked in the door.

"You might as well call me Miz Sehoy — everybody else does," David's mother told Ned and Becky. "But you will be my new sister," she smiled putting her arm around Jane Brown. "I have been so lonely since my sisters left. Jeanette went to France with her husband, General Milford, who's fighting for Napoleon, and my other sister Sophia moved down the rivet with her family to their big new plantation. Oh, it is so good to talk to a woman again!"

Sehoy was overjoyed when she found that Jane had been to boarding school in North Carolina. "I am so stupid about books," she said, making a face. "I should hate for my children to grow up as ignorant as their poor mama."

"Well, I'm not all that smart," said Jane, "but I can teach them to read and to write a nice hand. I'm glad to be of some use, since you've been so wonderful to us."

"That's settled then," said Sehoy gratefully. "Tomorrow we will arrange the schoolroom. I'm afraid I've let them run wild like the little savages they are. All but David." She laid her plump hand proudly on David's tanned arm. "He is our only scholar. His uncle has engaged a griffe named Percy to tutor little Alex and David."

"What is a griffe?" asked Becky.

"It is someone half-Negro, half-Indian," explained Sehoy. "Percy is from Mobile and is quite good with French and Spanish. But David can never get enough of learning. He has read half the books in his uncle's library already!"

"You can study with us, Ned," put in David. "That is, if you want to. My brother Billy can't stand books. When he's not breaking horses for father he's off in the forest hunting or trapping. He lives over at the racetrack."

Ned said he guessed he would like studying with David. "The few books Ma taught us from were just about wore out before they got burned up," he added. "I'd like mighty well to learn out of some new ones."

On the way over to Hickory Ground plantation next morning Ned asked David why his stepfather did not live at home with his family. David explained that all sorts of rough characters hung around the racetrack, men not fit to be around his mother and the children.

"You wouldn't believe how foulmouthed some of their talk is, especially when they're full of tafia. Billy likes to listen to their yarns, but the only thing I like about it is the horses. Dad has some real beauties!"

Nearly a month went by before Ned had a chance to meet Charles Weatherford and David's half-brother Billy. They arrived unexpectedly in the hallway one stormy night with a great stamping of muddy feet and shedding of wet raincoats. Ned's first thought was that Mr. Weatherford was just the way he had always pictured a typical Englishman, the kind his Pa had made fun of as "beef-eaters" and "bloody lobsterbacks." In the beginning he felt a little standoffish with this bluff, red-faced man with the great booming laugh. Ned soon found, however, that Mr. Weatherford was the kindest fellow imaginable. His children adored him, and the moment he stretched out in his big chair by the hearth the little ones swarmed all over him, searching in his pockets for the rock candy he always brought them.

After the children were sent to bed, Ned listened from his corner as Mr. Weatherford talked about his ranch. "Billy and I had planned to come home two weeks ago," he told them, "but Chief Menawa, that crazy horse stealer, and some of his warriors rode in from a trip up to the Cumberland and made camp right near the ranch, aimin' to sell me some of their horses. I know damn well they're stolen, and he knows I know it, but nobody's ever pinned anything on him and probably never will. He's slippery as an eel." He grunted and tapped out his pipe on the fender, relighting it with a stick from the fire. "Anyway, the upshot of it was, I didn't like to leave that rowdy bunch camped nearby, and I ended up trading with Menawa for some real fine horses."

"We think some of them are thoroughbred Andalusians," put in Billy, his dark eyes shining with excitement in the firelight. "We want them to build up our breeding stock."

Ned noticed that Billy Weatherford had more of an Indian look about him than David. He wore his straight black hair shoulder length and bound with a beaded headband and a red feather. What fascinated Ned most, though, was Billy's superb physique and the easy grace with which he moved. Ned thought he would give anything to have a set of muscles like that. He glanced in dismay at his puny arms and skinny legs. Billy caught the look and grinned. He seemed to notice everything.

"Dave told us you've been sick. Don't worry. We'll put some muscle on you when we get you out to the ranch. We've come to get Dave to help us break in these new horses."

Mr. Weatherford, however, put his foot down on this plan, to Ned's great disappointment. "I do need David, if he can tear himself away from his books for a while, but Ned here won't be much use to us, the shape he's in now. He'd better stay here and let Miz Sehoy fatten him up a bit and we'll take him with us next time."

It was surprising how lonely the big noisy house seemed when Mr. Weatherford and his tall sons rode off a few days later. The first week wasn't so bad because Ned still went over to Hickory Grove every morning to study with Alex and the tutor, and he had found some interesting books in the colonel's library.

Then little Alex had gotten sick, and the tutor, Mr. Francis, had called off lessons for a while. Ned supposed Mr. Francis was glad to get some time off to carry on his flirtation with the McGillivray's pretty Indian housemaid. But it left Ned at loose ends and he didn't know what to do with himself.

Finally Paro took pity on him and set him to work helping to build a new corn crib. Ned was good at carpentry — Pa had taught him while they were building the cabin — and he was pleased when Paro praised him and put him in charge of the men. When the job was finished, Ned got up nerve enough to ask Paro if someday when he had time he would show Ned how to make a bow and arrow.

Paro had a solution to that, too. He put Ned in the charge of

Chocco, the silent Indian boy who always followed David. "He's sad 'cause David's gone off without him," said Paro. "Chocco's fine with a bow and arrow, and he can bring down any kind of bird with a blowgun. He don't talk much," chuckled Paro, "but he do like to show off!"

Paro did not exaggerate. Chocco did not need to talk to demonstrate his skills. He lent Ned a bow, and they practiced until Ned could hit a mark at twenty paces. Then they went into the woods to find hickory to make a bow for Ned and lightwood for arrows. Ned was surprised to find that Indian boys of nine or ten could shoot fish with bows and arrows.

He was even more amazed at the way they used blowguns. These were made from canes six to eight feet long and were used to shoot birds and squirrels. These blowguns took an arrow about ten inches long. One end was sharp and the larger end was spirally grooved like an auger to fit inside the blowgun. Chocco would get right under a bird and shoot the arrow by blowing it out with his mouth. He never missed. But try as he would, it took Ned a long time to get his first bird.

Meanwhile, Ned was getting a good tan from the long hours in the sun, and the frequent swims in the river gave him a healthy appetite. He did not realize how much his appearance had changed until David came home a few weeks later, just as Ned was climbing up the bluff after a swim. "If it hadn't been for your yellow hair, I'd have thought you were one of the Indians!" laughed David.

"Well, back in Georgia a year ago I wouldn't have much liked that remark," Ned said thoughtfully, "but I know better now. It'll take me a long time to catch up with these Indian boys in swimming, shooting, or almost anything else."

"They have wonderful endurance, too" said David as they walked together toward the house. "Some of our runners — 'skunks', as we call them — can run for unbelievable distances. The Creeks have a good life in lots of ways. It's the only life Billy wants. Sometimes I wish I could be like him, or like Chocco there, just taking each day as it comes and not worrying about the future. I guess it's the books that make me think different — that, and talking to Uncle Alex. I kind of missed him when I was at the ranch."

Summer was over, and the sumac bushes were making red splashes in the woods before Ned finally got his chance to visit the ranch.

When Mr. Weatherford came home this time, he clapped Ned on the shoulder with a heavy hand and shouted happily, "Well, boy, you look a mite different now. You've put on some weight and shot up taller, too. We'll soon have to get Miz Sehoy to fix you up with a new pair of britches!"

Ned was always a little embarrassed by the big man's rough humor, though it was true that his homespun pants were about to burst their seams. "I'd sure admire to have a suit of buckskins," he ventured, "and some of those tall moccasins — is it 'stillipacos' you call them?"

"Righto! We'll get some of the Creek women to making an outfit for you. That's one of their jobs when they are housebound during the winter. Even some of the little girls can do nice beadwork."

Billy had not come home with his father this time because his favorite mare was in foal. Again there was much talk of horses as they sat around the fire on the chilly evenings, and Ned began to feel excited at the prospect of the new experiences in store for him. He did not know a great deal about horses but he was eager to learn. More than anything he longed to prove himself in the eyes of David and Billy, who rode as if they had been born knowing how.

Ned's first impression of the ranch was disappointing. After a grueling twenty-mile ride on a rough-gaited horse, he was looking forward to hot food and rest for his aching legs when Mr. Weatherford pulled up beside him and pointed eastward. "There's

Ikunchatta — that's Creek for Red Ground — over on the bluff there above the river. Tomorrow I'll show you the finest racetrack in the whole country."

Ned looked hard through the gathering dusk and could barely make out a huddle of low buildings in the middle of a vast empty field. In front of the longest building he could see men moving around a big fire. As they rode closer Ned could hear the babble of Muskogee talk, and he realized that all of the faces except one or two very dirty-looking white men were Indian.

The damp smell of the muddy river bayous had given way to the pervasive odor of horses and sweaty bodies mingled with the tantalizing whiff of roasting partridges and savory stew. The men were eating the birds with their fingers, and Ned noticed some of them pouring bear oil on the meat from hollowed-out containers made of cane which they wore strapped to their bodies.

The circle of swarthy faces turned towards them curiously as Mr. Weatherford introduced Ned as his young visitor from Georgia. Ned caught a gleam of pure hatred in the narrowed black eyes of a lank-haired, snaggle-toothed Indian staring at him across the fire. He barely caught the man's muttered words, "Damn Georgia pup!" when Mr. Weatherford turned away to question his foreman, and a moment later a well-directed stream of brown spittle landed near Ned's foot. Suddenly he felt strange and out of place in this dark, wild setting.

Then David and Billy were running toward him and everything was right again. There was much to ask and messages to give, with everyone talking at once. Then Old Tomo, the humpbacked cook, filled Ned's empty stomach and finally led him to a straw mattress in one of the long log buildings.

David slept here, too, but Billy had moved his bed to another building that was closer to the new colt he was training. Ned was almost staggering from weariness and the long, unaccustomed ride, but there was one question that bothered him. "Who was that snaggle-toothed fellow that cussed at me?" he asked David.

"Don't pay any mind to old Lupa," said David tolerantly. "He don't like anybody, but he's got a special hate for Georgians since they killed his brother last year."

"No reason he should take it out on me," said Ned. "I never did him any harm." But as he burrowed into the straw trying to ease his sore muscles into a comfortable position, he remembered a friend of his Pa back in Georgia saying, "The only good Injun's a dead Injun," and laughing while he said it. Maybe he'd have thought that way himself if he'd never come here and gotten to know David's folks.

"Lupa's a mean one all right," David was saying, "but he's good at his job. He's the best horse breaker we've got."

Ned found out how good Lupa was next morning when David showed him around the ranch. The whole top of the bluff as far as he could see was a network of log barns and pole corrals, and in all of them men were working with horses. Lupa was bossing a crew that was breaking in some of the wild horses that had been recently brought in.

The boys climbed on the fence to watch as a tall roan stallion reared and snorted around the circle, tossing two would-be riders in succession. Then Lupa took over, with his mouth a grim line and his wiry brown arms jerking the great head down with the cruel bit. In a few minutes the fight was over and the stallion was lathered and trembling. It was a fine display of horsemanship, and Ned wondered why he felt a little sad.

After a casual inspection of the feed lots, the grazing herd of pack ponies, and the special quarters for the brood mares, Ned and David came at last to the largest barn of all.

"These are my father's race horses," David explained as he swung open the big door to disclose a double row of box stalls. Ned was no expert, but he knew enough to gasp in amazement at the array of proudly arched necks and shining coats.

"Say! That's some fine horseflesh!" he exclaimed as they walked along the row. "This 'un would be my pick of 'em all, though," he said as they finally reached the last stall which housed a beautiful gray stallion.

"You're a good picker," laughed David. "Gray Boy is the sire of Billy's new colt that he's so crazy about. Billy's probably over at the racetrack with him now. We can get out through the back door."

At the racetrack they found not only Billy and the gray colt but his father and a visitor, a well-dressed elderly man with a big hooked nose and kind dark eyes. "Ned, this is our nearest neighbor, Mr. Abram Mordecai," Mr. Weatherford greeted them. "He runs a ferry and trading post down river. He likes to keep an eye on us when we try out our horses so he'll know where to put his money down in the Spring races."

Mr. Weatherford's great laugh rang out, and Mr. Mordecai echoed him good-naturedly. Soon they were deep in a discussion of the likeliest frontrunners of the new season.

Ned's attention began to wander, and he strolled along the fence toward the area where Billy was training his colt to obey voice signals. Billy was absorbed in his task, so Ned was the first to see the two Indian boys approaching from the far side of the cornfield that flanked the racetrack. They were half-leading, half dragging a pitiful, starved-looking colt about the size of the one Billy was training.

As Ned came closer, the boys pointed to the struggling colt and began chattering excitedly in Creek. Ned had been trying to learn the language, and he recognized the word "ulgee" for horseman and "echo tlooko" for horse, but the rest of it was beyond him. He held up his hand in protest. "Hey, slow down, boys! I don't speak your lingo yet." Then he ran to the fence and yelled, "Billy, can you come here? I can't make out what these boys are saying."

Billy strolled toward them laughing, but he stopped when he saw the colt's condition. "Where did you find him? What happened?"

The boys rapidly told their story and Billy relayed it to Ned. The colt had been accidentally left behind by Menawa's horsemen when it became entangled in thick brush down in the big swamp. "Some of those drivers," Billy explained, "when they make a gather of wild horses, will tire them out by driving the poor creatures back and forth through heavy mud in the swamps until the fight's all out of them — makes them easier to control. I guess that's how they came to overlook this little fellow."

Billy's face showed what he thought of this practice. He turned back to the Indian boys. "Take him over to that first barn where Old Tomo's got the young stuff. I'll tell my Pa to give you something for bringing him in."

As the boys struggled off with the colt, Billy shrugged his shoulders and muttered, "Old Tomo's a pretty good horse doctor, but I'm afraid that one's not going to make it."

"Do you suppose I could help Tomo?" asked Ned eagerly. He had great sympathy for the little colt. After all, he knew how it felt to be brought to a strange place all battered and bruised.

Billy agreed that Ned might be of some use to Old Tomo. "I've just started with my colt and I hate to break off right now or I'd come with you."

The humpbacked cook shook his head over the jagged and bleeding cuts and felt carefully along the colt's legs with his probing fingers. "Ain't nothing broken or sprained. He jes' might make it."

"Can I help take care of him?" Ned pleaded.

Old Tomo looked relieved. "You sure kin, boy. I'll give you some salve to use and show you how to make corn meal poultices, an' the job's all yours. I got more to do already than I kin ever get aroun' to."

At first the little colt lunged against the walls and rolled its eyes in fear, but Ned kept talking to it softly as he fed it until finally it stopped trembling and allowed itself to be touched. Under Old Tomo's careful instructions Ned learned to mix the healing herbs with warm corn meal and to tie the poultices over the worst places.

They kept coming off, of course, whenever the colt thrashed around, but in the end the little creature seemed to reconcile itself to Ned's voice and hands. When David came to call Ned to supper, he found him asleep in the straw with his arm still holding a poultice in place on the sleeping colt.

As the cuts and scratches began to heal, Ned noticed that the colt was beginning to respond to his presence. It would nuzzle his shoulder and blow softly into his cupped palms, and when he finally let it out into the corral it would follow him around and come to his whistle. It was soon tacitly agreed around the ranch that the newcomer rightly belonged to Ned.

"What'll you call him?" asked David one day.

"I thought maybe a Creek name. Doesn't 'chatta' mean red?"

"Yes. You know the name of this ranch is Ikun-chatta, meaning red ground, and the Creek name of my great-uncle, Chief Red Shoes, is 'Stillipaco-chatta.' Your colt will be a brighter color when he's full grown so that should be a good name," replied David. "Say, why don't you ask Billy to help you train him? He'll be big enough for you to ride before you know it."

Ned was already beginning to worry about his own riding ability. He could not help envying David and Billy's effortless skill. He wasn't good enough and he knew it, but he was determined to learn by the time Chatta was ready to be ridden. "Pick me out a horse to practice on," he asked David one day, "one that's broke in enough so I won't make a fool of myself. I've never had a chance to learn how, or not real good anyhow."

Accordingly, next morning David told Lupa to saddle Silver for Ned. "He's gentle and shouldn't give you any trouble," he said. "I've ridden him lots of times because he has nice gaits." With a friendly parting wave, David strolled off toward the larger barn where he was helping with the latest string of horses brought in by Menawa's men.

Ned liked Silver's looks and stroked the gelding's slender nose with an appreciative hand before mounting. What happened next was totally unexpected. One moment Ned was in the saddle, the next moment the tall horse was rearing and bucking frantically and Ned was *flying* through the air. For a few seconds he lay stunned in the dust of the ring. Then as he slowly picked himself up, rubbing his bruised posterior, he heard a few subdued chuckles from the old hands. Through Ned's rage and pain he caught a gleam of pure malevolence from the black slits of Lupa's eyes as he passed him at the barn door.

Old Tomo gave him some evil-smelling stuff to smear over his bruises and looked dubious when Ned told him he had been thrown by Silver. "That don't seem right to me. Silver, you say? Why, he's gentle as a lamb."

"That's what David said, too, but my behind says different," muttered Ned.

"Was it Lupa saddled him fer ya?" asked Tomo, and at Ned's affirmative nod Tomo scuttled hurriedly toward the door with his crablike gait. Ned remembered Billy's telling him that Old Tomo had been a top rider before his back had been injured in a fall from a wild horse.

In a few seconds Tomo hurried back leading Silver by the reins. "Got there jest in time," he panted. "Seemed like Lupa was in a might big hurry to take off Silver's saddle. Let's see if my hunch is right."

He raised the saddle carefully and ran an exploratory finger under the leather. "Aah, looky here now!" he grunted with satisfaction, pulling out a handful of hard, spiny cockleburs. Tomo nodded his graying head and rubbed his chin. "Well, boy, looks like ol' Lupa's got it in fer you, and thet ain't good. Lupa learnt his meanness from Savannah Jack, who was his master before he came here. I spec' you've heard of him even way off there in Georgy."

Ned nodded. "I once heard my Pa say he was the cruellest, most bloodthirsty man who ever lived."

"That's him all right," agreed Tomo. "Him and his Pa were both white men raised by Indians. Jack's as bad as his half-brother Simon Girty, who fought for the British up north in the Ohio country where they was both raised. Well, Lupa's kinfolks come south with Savannah Jack, and now all of 'ems been killed by Georgians 'cept Lupa."

"He scares me," admitted Ned. "His eyes don't look human."

At Old Tomo's suggestion, Ned decided to saddle his own horses henceforward and to practice his riding early in the morning before the other hands were about.

"Any good horseman knows how to make and care for his own gear," said Tomo. "We've got plenty of spare rawhide in the tack room. I'll show you how to fashion a braided lasso and a hackamore."

Ned looked bewildered and Old Tomo laughed. "Don't be ashamed to ask questions — just so you don't ask no favors from Lupa. A hackamore's nothin' but a head stall without a bit. You'll want to start Chatta off just learnin' how to walk around the ring behind a lead rope. It'll be a long time before you'll want to put a bit in his mouth."

That was the beginning of Ned's intensive training in horsemanship. He used his eyes and ears to pick up bits of lore from the experienced handlers, and gradually he became expert at grooming and caring for the saddle stock. Ned beamed with pride when Old Tomo told him that he had good hands. "That's important, boy, an' don't you never forget it!"

They had been at the corral watching Lupa's quick mastery of another fractious wild horse, and again Ned wondered if it were necessary to be so brutal with the animal. Finally he confided to Tomo, "Seems like Lupa jerks the horse's head down so hard with that Spanish bit that it don't do the horse's mouth no good."

"Jes' so," the old man replied. "That's the very reason the master don't let Lupa handle his race horses. A real fine horse has got a tender mouth an' takes better to gentlin' like you're doin' with Chatta. Wouldn't surprise me a bit if one of these days you'd come to find out you had yourse'f a race horse there. 'Course it's early days yet . . ."

Billy agreed with Tomo that Chatta had interesting possibilities. "Notice the arch to his tail and his neck, and those long flowing tail hairs. Unless I miss my guess, that horse is part Arabian. They don't get real big, but they're fast and graceful. But then, you're not so big yourself!" He laughed and punched Ned's shoulder, and Ned grinned.

"Well, whatever he is, he sure suits me!"

Ned had fallen into the habit of watching Billy's training sessions with his gray colt, Arrow, so that he would learn more about how to train Chatta.

When Paro came to the ranch one day from Hickory Ground with word that the Indians of Little Tallassee were planning their winter hunt, it was not hard for Ned to turn down the invitation to join them, though he loved hunting and had often gone with his father. "I'd like to go if it wasn't for Chatta, but come see for yourself, Paro, how good he's lookin'. If you'd seen him when they first brought him in."

Paro's smile was understanding. "I'll tell your Ma and Becky how well you're looking. Master David, now, he's itchin' to get back to his books, but I can see you're in no mind to join him right away!"

"Tell Ma I promise I'll study extra hard when I get back. I'll even study some out here if she'll send me some books. But explain to 'em how it is, Paro, please! I jus' can't leave now."

Ned hated to tell David good-bye the next morning, and a few days later when Billy was persuaded to lead one of the groups on the winter hunt, Ned was disappointed. But still he did not change his mind. "Chatta's answering to voice signals almost as good as Arrow now," he told Billy. "By the time you all get back, Tomo says he'll be ready for the bit. 'N' then, by golly, I'll challenge you to a race, though you'll prob'ly beat the socks off me!"

So many of the Ikunchatta men joined the hunt that the ranch was left with only a skeleton crew. As a result, Ned was too busy to feel lonely. It was a great relief to him when Lupa joined the exodus. There had been no incidents since the cocklebur episode, but Ned could feel the man's hatred whenever he was around him.

It was during these short winter days when Ned was helping Old Tomo groom the race horses that he got to know Mr. Weatherford better. "You've got quite a way with the horses, lad," he boomed at Ned one day. "Come over to my office when you've finished here an' I'll show you something." Mr. Weatherford's office opened out of the small log trading post beyond the racing stable, and its window had a view of the Alabama River. This was Ned's first visit, and he looked around curiously. On the walls above the desk and the bunk bed in the corner were colored prints of race horses. One picture was of fox hunters in red coats jumping a fence. On the desk was a little statue of a horse carved out of wood.

Seeing Ned's interest, Mr. Weatherford stroked it gently with his big hand. "An old Indian carved this for me. It's a likeness of my finest racer, who broke his leg and had to be put away. I never hope to see his like again."

His voice was gruff with feeling, and Ned sympathized. He knew how he would feel if something like that happened to Chatta. Then Mr. Weatherford opened a chest and brought out a big book full of pictures of horses with all their pedigrees and bloodlines. As he turned the pages, he talked of famous horses he had seen or heard of as a boy in England and Ireland, and how he hoped one day to develop a line of his own that would beat anything in the old country.

"I learned about horses from my father — he was a trainer back in England — and I know there's wonderful speed and endurance in some of our horses that come from the Arkansas plains. Now if we could just cross that tough stock with a blooded sire from England, like these in here . . ." He touched the book and gazed off into space above Ned's head as if he saw a picture in his mind of people coming from everywhere to praise the American champion.

Ned had seen a look like that before. It had been on his father's face when he had talked of the great plantation he would build some day in the new lands. Ma's one desire, he knew, was to get back to her kinfolks in North Carolina, and Ned had realized all along that his stay in the Creek Nation was only a temporary one.

Colonel McGillivray had promised to furnish the family with guides to Mobile in the Spring when the furs from the winter hunt were ready to be shipped abroad. He would arrange for his ship to put the Browns off at Wilmington on the Carolina coast near Jane's home.

As he looked out of the window at the wide Alabama River, Ned asked himself whether he really wanted to go back, just when Chatta was getting his growth. He knew he'd have to face it when the time came, but for now he would try to keep his mind on becoming a first-rate horse trainer.

Mr. Weatherford gave him some good advice about how to get Chatta ready for a saddle. "I guess you've noticed that lots of the Indians ride bareback, but the best of 'em use riding pads. You'll want to get Chatta used to the feel of one. It's no more than a tanned robe held in place by a wide, soft strap or cinch. Later, Old Tomo can show you how to bend and shape green wood into a saddle and stirrups, and then cover them both with damp rawhide. We make most everything we need right here on the place," he said proudly, "though occasionally we do take in some Spanish saddles or other gear in trade."

Ned thanked Mr. Weatherford and hurried back to beg Old Tomo to show him how to make a riding pad. By the time Billy got back from the hunt, Ned wanted to surprise him by having Chatta ready to ride. He had already gotten him used to taking the bit, and he was eager to begin the next step.

This consisted of first walking the colt around the ring, with Ned's hand lightly holding the riding pad in place. Finally there came the glorious moment when Ned slid his leg across the pad, keeping up a stream of small talk so the little horse would not be frightened: "That's the way, Chatta. Don't be scared. It's just me, boy. C'mon, now, we're ready to go!"

With that, they were off, and to Ned's great satisfaction, Chatta seemed ready to accept this strange new burden on his back. He twisted and plunged a bit at first and tossed his head questioningly, but Ned kept up his flow of talk until Chatta was trotting smoothly around the corral as if he had been doing it for months.

The crowning triumph of the day came just as Ned completed the last lap of his ride. Suddenly he heard the unmistakable sound of the returning hunters. He had drawn up to the corral gate and was proudly patting the wet and glistening arch of Chatta's neck when Billy ran up and yelled out enviously, "Well, by gum, if you haven't got ahead of me! But that's great, Ned, real great! Just gimme a few days of work with Arrow and we'll be ridin' out together explorin' the country!"

The short winter days that followed were full of new and exciting experiences. The two boys hunted small game, usually with bows and arrows which Billy, like Ned, preferred to guns. Also Billy showed Ned how to set traps and how to prepare his pelts for curing. When the pelts were ready, Ned traded some of them for a beaded buckskin jacket and a fur hat to go with the new britches the colonel had sent him by Paro. Ned felt that he cut a fine figure indeed as he and Billy rode along the wooded trail toward Hickory Ground on Ned's first trip back to Miz Sophy's since leaving for Ikunchatta five months ago. It was a good homecoming. Becky teased him by pretending not to recognize him. Ma felt of Ned's new iron-hard muscles and claimed he had grown at least five inches taller. Then Billy's little brothers capered around admiring his new outfit and making a big fuss over Chatta. Soon Miz Sophy was dishing out a wonderful smelling pork roast and Ned was trying to remember how to eat with proper table manners and not spear the meat with his knife like the Indian ranch hands.

Ma was worried about Ned's missing the chance for schooling with Alex and David's tutor, but she finally agreed to let him return to Ikunchatta if he would borrow some of Colonel McGillivray's books to take back with him to study. Paro told Ned he would help him make some Indian saddlebags out of wide strips of soft leather with long fringes on each end. He could use them to carry his books.

Becky hung over him while he worked, full of questions as usual. "Listen, Ned, Rosie and Lizzie have been teaching me how to make patterns with beads and dyed quills. Let me put some decorations on those flap things for you. Please!"

"Well, I guess so, if you want to," Ned agreed. "Just so you don't mess 'em up."

Soon all that remained to be done was to visit Hickory Ground with David and enlist Colonel McGillivray's help with the books. On the colonel's advice, Ned agreed without much enthusiasm that every young man should read a translation of Homer and the essays of the Greek philosophers. However, he was really excited when David discovered in the library a book on the care and treatment of horses. With this and Mr. Weatherford's stud books, Ned was sure he could learn more about his fascinating new interest. In the back of his mind the idea was forming that maybe some day he could learn to breed his own horses.

When Billy and Ned returned to Ikunchatta, they found preparations already under way for the Spring races. After the first spell of warm weather, increasing numbers of visitors began to arrive by canoe or pack train, and always the talk was of horses and racing. Lupa spread the word among the hands that Savannah Jack had a black stallion named Satan that he would bet on to beat Gray Boy. Abram Mordecai came over often and dropped hints that he just might have a surprise entry of his own if his plans worked out. There were unfounded rumors that a wealthy Spanish merchant from Mobile planned to enter a horse, and it was certain that there would be entries from Pensacola.

One day an Indian runner arrived from the Oconee River country with a message that a rich Georgia planter would like to enter his best racing horse if Mr. Weatherford could provide him with safe conduct through the Creek Nation. "They come from further off every year," Mr. Weatherford said to Ned, who was looking through the horse books in the chest. "One of these days our races will be known all over the South. I just hope all these owners will bring fat purses with them!"

His big laugh rang out, and Ned laughed with him. He no longer felt awkward around the big man and lately had been spending more time in the office studying the stud books. He was a little discouraged at how much there was to learn and how vast was his own ignorance despite all his efforts.

Race day was set for mid-March, and as the time approached, the excitement intensified. Coins of any sort were scarce at the ranch. Most of the hands merely swapped their furs or services for credit at the trading post, and many hard drinkers were habitually in debt for tafia. As post time approached, however, many a cherished possession, such as a bone-handled knife or an ornamented piece of riding gear or beaded head dress, was wagered on one of the favorites.

One early morning as Ned was taking Chatta for his accustomed ride through a nearby woods, he discovered that Lupa had not forgotten him. As he approached a spot where the trail rounded a dense canebrake, there was a sudden loud clash of metal and at the same time a bright flash of color as something on a stick was thrust out in front of Chatta's head.

If Ned had not been alerted by a brief glimpse of movement out of the corner of his eye, he might have taken a bad fall when the little horse shied in terror and plunged headlong through the low-hanging limbs. As it was, he barely managed to keep his seat, and he had to spend a long time stroking and calming the frightened animal. He had no proof of the prankster's identity, of course, but it was the sort of trick Lupa would pull, and Ned made a silent vow to be more watchful than ever.

Though Ned made no wagers, he loyally supported Mr. Weatherford's famous Gray Boy, as did most of the handlers. Ned had grown attached to the beautiful animal on the few occasions when Old Tomo, under the pressure of his multitude of dudes, had allowed him to help with the grooming. "Mr. Weatherford's mighty particular 'bout this horse," Tomo had claimed. "Generally he don't like nobody but me to handle him." Since the day Mr. Weatherford had commented that Ned had "good hands," Tomo had been less averse to sharing some of his duties with his young helper.

Never in his fondest dreams, however, had Ned pictured himself on Gray Boy's back. That privilege belonged to a small copper-skinned boy called Weenoma, who exercised him daily and who planned to ride him in the race. Consequently, when Mr. Weatherford appeared at Gray Boy's stall one day with a long face and snapped out abruptly, "Think you can ride that horse, boy?" Ned's mouth dropped open and his grooming brush fell from his limp hand.

"Me!" he exclaimed when he could get his mouth shut. "Ride Gray Boy? Gosh, sir, I . . . Gosh!" He looked at the big horse in wonder. Then his hand went up tentatively to stroke the great curving neck, and the horse snorted gently in appreciation. "Well, mebbe I could, at that! Me and him is friends. But why me? What's happened to Weenoma?"

"Sprained his wrist, dammit!" Mr. Weatherford jerked out, "and the race just three days off! You're small enough — Billy's too heavy — and your seat's good. I been watching you off and on, son, and Gray Boy takes to you. Mind you now, I don't want his mouth ruint, even if you have to give him his head a mite. I won't have him whipsawed!"

"Oh, I'd never do that, sir, no matter what!"

"No, I don't believe you would. You've got good hands, like I always said. Think he can do it, Tomo?"

Old Tomo hunched his crooked back and put his head on one side judiciously. Finally he nodded approval. "Worth a try," he muttered. "After dark we'll slip him out to the far end of the track, let him walk him around a spell . . . get the feel of him. If Gray Boy don't toss him off, Ned can start workin' him tomorrow at daybreak 'fore anybody gets wind of this. D'you suppose Weenoma can keep his mouth shut?"

"I'll see to that," growled Mr. Weatherford. "The wrappings

on his wrist don't show under his jacket, and I'll tell him not to circulate among the men."

Thus began Ned's greatest adventure. He used the same tactics with Gray Boy that had worked so well with Chatta — first leading him around with his arm resting on the pommel as he murmured to him in a low voice, and finally easing weight gently into the light racing saddle. Gray Boy did not even flick his ears, and Ned gave a great sigh of relief. "Me an' you are goin' to make it, Gray Boy," he said softly. "We're gonna run us a race."

It was impossible, of course, for the change of riders to remain a secret very long in a close community like Ikunchatta. Inevitably some sharp-eyed early riser spotted Ned on Gray Boy's back on the morning before the race. The momentous news spread rapidly in the keyed up atmosphere of race day eve, but by this time Ned was confident of Gray Boy's response. As he felt the powerful muscles move beneath his slender thighs, he could imagine what it must be like to be an army officer leading a cavalry charge into battle on a great war horse. In a way, tomorrow would be like a war. He hoped to goodness Lupa wouldn't try to make trouble.

Late in the afternoon the visiting party from Little Tallassee arrived, with Paro like an elderly pied piper surrounded by a chattering flock of children on their tough little Indian ponies. Mrs. McGillivray was too frail to make the rough trip, but Ned quickly spotted Ma and Miz Sehoy as they laughingly brushed the dust from their finery.

As he ran to greet them he caught a glimpse of Colonel McGillivray's noble profile in the center of an admiring throng, with David at his side. The colonel was dressed in an elegant gold-braided Spanish uniform, and Ned thought it made him look like a king. Mr. Weatherford had turned the ranch hands out of one of the bunkhouses and had it scoured out so the women and children would have a clean place to shelter.

Tomorrow this whole place would be full of strangers coming in from everywhere, Ned thought, and he'd be out there on Gray Boy with all those eyes watching him. It gave him the jitters. He shivered, and for a moment he felt a pang of loneliness, though he was sure his family and all his new friends would be pulling for him. Uneasy in his mind about Lupa, Ned decided to bed down just outside Gray Boy's stall. He would sleep with one ear open as he had learned to do when he had gone hunting with Pa.

The night passed without incident, however, and Ned awoke to find the big stallion gazing down at him with a mildly questioning look. He jumped up with a laugh and decided to give Gray Boy a quick grooming before Old Tomo arrived to supervise the final feeding. Then he would go to Mr. Weatherford's office for his last minute instructions and to put on what the big Englishman described as his "silks." All this really meant was that Ned would exchange his fringed buckskin jacket for a light green silk vest which gave his arms more freedom. Most of the riders would have bare torsos, but Mr. Weatherford liked to do things with style.

Ned found him nervously pacing the office and pulling at his mustache, but he made a visible effort to appear confident when Ned came In. "Now you just give him his head, boy," he said for what must have been the tenth time. "That horse knows more about racing than you do. You just look out for a little hole in the pack and he'll take you right through it."

Ned submitted to these rambling instructions with good grace, hoping with all his heart that he would not make any mistakes. When he came out again into the bright Spring sunshine, he decided to take a quick look at the race track. He was amazed at the size of the crowd. Ned figured just about everybody in the Creek Nation must be there, only he hadn't known there were that many people in this wilderness country.

He saw Abram Mordecai standing beside his wife, a handsome

motherly looking woman with light copper-colored skin and slightly negroid features. Ned figured she must be a griffe, like his former tutor, Mr. Francis. One of Mr. Mordecai's sons was riding his father's brand new spotted horse that he claimed had some Arabian blood. Ned liked the look of the horse, but he had noticed the boy was a clumsy rider with heavy hands.

Savannah Jack's entry, Satan, was the horse Ned was really worried about, and he scanned the crowd in an effort to spot Satan's rider. Finally he saw him over by the fence in a huddled conversation with Ned's old enemy, Lupa. Ned longed to know what they were talking about. He wished he could get close enough to hear, but they were bound to spot him in his bright green silks, and they were probably talking in Creek anyway.

Then he saw Becky and David's sisters holding the new dolls Paro had carved for them, and suddenly he had an idea. "Come over here a moment, Becky," he called when he caught her eye. "Bring your friends if you like." Then he quickly outlined his idea, describing Lupa and Satan's rider to the girls but warning them not to look in that direction.

"I need to know what they're saying but I don't know the Muskogee lingo like you do. Now if you girls will just wander over that way and put your heads together like you're playin' with your dolls, they won't pay you any mind. Then you can come over and tell me."

Becky giggled with delight. "Oh, this is fun! I'll be your spy like I was when we were in the Autossee town. C'mon, Rosie, make like we're whispering to our babies!" The three conspirators strolled off with an exaggerated look of innocence.

Ned waited in the barn with barely suppressed impatience for his spies to report. Old Tomo was chuckling over Ned's strategy. "Girls and doll babies, now. Who'd of thought of that?"

Then Becky was back, with the others panting breathlessly

behind her "That snaggle-toothed man sure talks ugly!" she said in disgust. "Ma'd have a fit if she knew I'd heard words like he uses!"

"Ah, come on, Sis! I haven't got all day!" Ned moaned.

"Well, Captain Ned, the enemy's gonna try to push you into the fence," said Becky, drawing herself up proudly with a salute. "He said lots more, but that was the main thing. He's countin' on you not bein' a 'sperienced rider — so you be careful, Ned! I don't like his looks!"

Chief Alexander McGillivray was given the honor of firing his pistol to start the great race, and an important looking Spanish official from Pensacola stood beside him holding Mr. Weatherford's expensive imported timepiece. Then the pistol banged and they were off. The crowd shouted and jostled, children shoved and screamed, and the bright dark eyes of the women shone eagerly from under calico bonnets or fancy Creek head dresses.

On the first lap of the quarter-mile track, the twelve starters stayed fairly even, with the riders hanging back slightly to save their mounts for the final burst of speed in the crucial fourth lap. Ned's nervousness began to ease a little as he felt the thrust of Gray Boy's powerful leg muscles. "That's it, boy! Keep a-going. That's fine!" he exulted, remembering to keep a loose rein and give the big horse his head.

By the end of the second lap, the Spanish horses from Mobile and Pensacola were falling behind. They were speedy and graceful but lacked the power of Gray Boy, Satan, or Mordecai's part-Arabian. The Georgia planter's chestnut was challenging now, but Ned sensed it was too early for the big push. The Mordecai boy was whipping his horse ahead of the chestnut. The poor fool, Ned thought, his horse couldn't last long at that rate. Sure enough, on the third lap the Mordecai horse began dropping behind.

With his attention momentarily on the contest between the Mordecai horse and the chestnut, it took Ned a few seconds to realize that his own mount was under attack. "Watch it now, Gray Boy. Watch that black," he said more to himself than to the horse. For the wily Gray Boy, with two winning races to his credit, needed no warning. Three times Satan's rider tried deliberately to force the gray stallion into the fence.

On the first try Gray Boy fell back as his inexperienced rider instinctively pulled hard on the reins. "Doggonit!" groaned Ned. "That's just what he wants me to do. He won't trap us again. Watch out now, boy!" Next time Ned was ready, and instead of falling back, he flicked Gray Boy into a burst of speed and got safely away. On the last try they almost didn't make it, as the chestnut's rider frantically whipped his mount into a final challenge that left Ned no room to maneuver.

Then at the last second the tired chestnut was dropping back again and Ned was through the gap. Now it was Satan and Gray Boy, neck and neck, and for the first time Ned used his quirt but more in excitement than anger. He trusted Gray Boy, but he had to have that final burst of speed. He leaned far over the great neck with his lips close to Gray Boy's ear. "You've got to do it. Beat him now, beat him!"

Then suddenly it was over, and Gray Boy had won. In a tired haze Ned saw Satan's rider throw down his whip in a gesture of rage. Vaguely he remembered Tomo's instructions to trot Gray Boy around to cool him off. Then as he turned back toward the starting post, full awareness surged over him, and he gave a great whoop of pure joy, "We've won, Gray Boy! You're the champion!"

The next thing he knew, he was being pulled bodily from the horse's back. Billy was hugging him, and Becky was squealing and tugging at his arm. Mr. Weatherford's round face had a beatific smile, and everybody was yelling and shouting in a perfect bedlam of sound.

Ned loved every minute of it. When he led Gray Boy over to

receive the victor's wreath from the hands of Colonel McGillivray, his heart felt ready to burst.

He slept dreamlessly through the long night of carousal and celebration, of drunken quarrels over wagers, and noisy preparations for departure. By mid-morning only the family party was left, and they were trying to round up the excited children who were busily exploring the premises.

Ned was still walking on air in the exaltation of Gray Boy's victory.

The blow fell without warning. Ned had no premonition when Mr. Weatherford beckoned him into his office where Colonel McGillivray was seated beside the desk. "Sit down, son," the chief said, waving Ned into the chair beside him. "Something has come up that we need to talk over with you." As Ned sat down he continued, "Senor Carvaiho, who was here yesterday from Pensacola, has informed me that Captain Malcolm's ship has already arrived from Scotland and is awaiting our shipment of furs and other items. Of course, you know what that means." He smiled sadly.

Ned could not meet the colonel's eyes. Tears burned behind his eyelids. "Yes, sir," he murmured finally. "I know Ma's set on going, but I . . ."

He could not go on, and Colonel McGillivray said firmly, "I know you'd like to stay here at the ranch. Charles tells me how well you've done here, and I know how you must feel about leaving your colt and your friends here."

Ned swallowed and hung his head, "Y-yes, sir."

"On the other hand," resumed the colonel, "There's this to consider. I can furnish protection for your mother and Becky to Pensacola, and Captain Malcolm is a fine man who knew my father Lachlan in the old days. But Ned, your mother is still a young and attractive woman and Becky is just a child. What do you think your father would want you to do?"

Ned looked up for the first time and squared his chin. "I understand, sir. I guess they'll need me. I'll go."

It had all happened so quickly, Ned thought, but maybe it was best that way. He had only time to throw his few possessions into his new fringed saddlebags and to pay a hurried last visit to Chatta. If he'd had longer to think about it, he knew he couldn't have brought himself to leave. As he turned away from Chatta's stall, David came up and walked silently with him along the path above the river toward the departing group who were mounting their horses at the head of the trail.

"I'll say good-bye here," said David suddenly. "I'm staying on a few days, you know, to help clean up. But if you're worried about Chatta . . ."

"That's just it!" Ned mourned. "I had such big plans for him, an' he was comin' along so good. He might even be a famous racer, an' now I won't ever know."

"If you'd like me to carry on for you, Ned, I'll do my best to train him," David promised.

"Thanks, David, I know you will, an' I'd like that," said Ned gratefully.

David gazed down the river with a far away look in his eyes. "Billy doesn't ever want to leave this place, but you know how I feel, Ned. I want to live in the white man's world some day and get a real college education so I can come back and help my people. Who knows? I might even come to see you in North Carolina one of these days!" He grinned and lifted his hand in farewell.

"Yeah, who knows?" agreed Ned. "Well, so long, David," and Ned turned his back on the red bluff of Ikunchatta and walked down the hill to where the others waited.

THAT MIGHT HAVE BEEN the end of Ned Brown's story if it had not been for a momentous event in the history of the Creek

Nation the next year. In 1790 President George Washington, eager to promote friendship between the Creeks and their southern neighbors, sent Colonel Marinus Willet to the Alabama country to persuade the Creek leader, Chief McGillivray, to visit him in New York City. He promised to make Alexander a general in the United States Army, the first ever appointed by an American President.

McGillivray's party set out from Little Tallassee on horseback — the two Negroes Paro and Jonah, young David Tate and his cousin Lachlan Durant, and twenty-four warriors and chiefs of the Creeks. In all the towns along the way the citizens turned out to welcome and honor them, in Stone Mountain, Georgia, in Richmond and Fredricksburg, Virginia — but in Guilford Courthouse, North Carolina, the welcome was a very special one.

Citizens lining the main street to watch the parade of chiefs, many of them in their bright ceremonial garments and elaborate head dresses, were surprised to see a woman suddenly run out into the street and fling her arms around Chief McGillivray. It was Jane Brown, with Becky right beside her. Through her tears and laughter, Jane turned toward the crowd of curious spectators clustering behind her and explained, "This wonderful man rescued my children and me from slavery and treated us as members of his family for nearly a year. It is thanks to him that I am back among you and restored to my parents."

Ned did not hear his mother's speech. He was looking at a prancing roan horse with a graceful arched neck and a long flowing tail. On its back was a tall boy with very blue eyes and a wide grin on his suntanned face.

"David!" yelled Ned. "And is it really . . ." At the sound of the familiar voice, the roan turned his head and nickered softly, and Ned ran over to stroke Chatta's slender nose.

David dismounted, laughing. "He's all yours! I just rode him home for you. We'll be going on by ship at the next town, and I'm to stay in New York to go to school, remember?"

Ned nodded happily and did not know what he answered. His mind was busy with dreams again of the great racing stable he would have some day, maybe over beyond the mountains. He would find a blooded mare for Chatta and start a new breed . . . He turned back to David. "Gosh! How can I thank you?"

"You already have," smiled David.

Historical Notes on "The Creek Captives"

Creeks, or Muscogees: *Memoir of Travels in the Creek Nation* **by Gen. LeClerc Milfort, R. R. Donnely, Chicago, 1956**

"The English gave them the name Creeks from the many rivers. They lived on the Missouri, then the Ohio, always chasing their enemies, the Alabamos. Later they came to the Alabama River at Montgomery and founded Autauga and Coosawda also. The Tuskegees settled in the forks of the Coosa and Tallapoosa where Fort Toulouse was later built by the French. The Creeks were later joined by Uchees from Savannah, some Shawnees from Florida, and a branch of the Natchez Indians also. In 1783 they founded the town of Souvanogee where Savannah Jack lived."

Captivity in the Autossee Town: *History of Alabama,* **A.J. Pickett, Birmingham, 1962 reprint**

"The bloody Coosawdas often took captives under their chief, Captain Isaacs. In 1792 they took Elizabeth Baker and danced around the scalps of her mother, father, brothers and sisters daily, hung on their council house. Charles Weatherford ransomed her and placed her with his wife Sehoy, and she finally was returned to her friends."

The Brown Family: *History of Alabama,* A.J. Pickett

"Some years before 1190, the Creeks killed Joseph Brown, from Guildford, North Carolina, captured his wife and children, and brought them to the Nation. Colonel McGillivray paid their ransom and kept them over a year . . . . On June 1, 1190, during McGillivray's march to New York, when his party arrived in North Carolina, all on horseback and with packhorses and three wagons in which rode 26 warriors with four on horseback, Mrs. Brown rushed through the large assembly, and with a great flood of tears greeted Alexander with words of admiration of his character and gratitude for saving her and her children's lives."

David Tate: *Reminiscences of Creek or Muskogee Indians,* T.S. Woodward, 1939, Weatherford Printing Press, Tuscaloosa, Alabama.

"David Tate was the son of Princess Sehoy of the Wind tribe and Colonel John Tate, the last agent the English had among the Creeks. He was a man of fine sense, great firmness, very kind to those with whom he was intimate, and charitable with strangers.

The Muscogee or Creek Indians, **Dr. M. E. Tarvin,** Galveston, Texas, 1939

"David Tate was good, wealthy, and distinguished."

Blow Guns: *Tales of Talladega,* Grace Jemison, Paragon Press, Montgomery, Ala., 1949

These blowguns and other objects made from cane are fully described here.

General Alexander McGillivray: *History of Alabama,* A.J. Pickett

"Alexander was generous to the distressed, whom he always sheltered and fed and protected from the brutalities of his red brethren. One of his many noble traits was his unbounded hospitality to friends and foes."

Muskogee or Creek Indians, Dr. M.E. Tarvin

"Alexander McGillivray was six feet tall, erect, a charming entertainer with a bold and lofty head, long and tapering fingers. He wrote rapidly. He was often taciturn unless he was interested but was always polite. He often wore British or Spanish uniform, and later his American one."

Charles Weatherford: *History of Alabama,* A.J. Pickett

"The Weatherfords always had fine horses, and William's father Charles was a celebrated patron of the Alabama turf who laid out the first race track in Alabama. Horse thieves from the Georgia frontier often tried out their stolen horses there."

Ikunchatta: *Milestones in Alabama's Pathway,* Peter Brannon

"Ikunchatta Bluff was Weatherford's Bluff until 1814. In fact, he owned all the bluff from the north end of Court Street in Montgomery to the lower end of Maxwell Field."

William (Billy) Weatherford, or Red Eagle: *History of Alabama,* T.M. Owen, S.J. Clark, Chicago, 1921

"William Weatherford was born near Coosada in Lowndes County, the son of a wealthy Englishman, Charles Weatherford and Sehoy, a Creek princess of the Wind tribe. He was a proficient horseman and athlete and an eloquent speaker. He had a large plantation on the Alabama River. He was influenced toward war with whites by Tecumseh, but his own brothers tried to influence him against war. . . . He tried to prevent the butchery at Fort Mims."

Savannah Jack: *Reminiscences of the Creek or Muskogee Indians,* T.S. Woodward

In Pennsylvania the Shawnees captured and raised a white boy named John Hague who married a Uchee woman and had children by her. He also raised two illegitimate sons by a captured white woman named Girty. Savannah Jack was his youngest son by the Uchee woman. Pickett calls him "the most bloodthirsty, fiendish, and cruel white man who ever lived."

Abram Mordecai: *Milestones Along Alabama's Pathway,* **Peter Brannon**

"Abram Mordecai, a Pennsylvania Dutchman and a Jew, lived two miles west of Line Creek, in 1783 in Montgomery. He built a pole trading house daubed with mud to look European." Pickett says his wife was Indian-Negro.

Sam Dale and the Long-tailed Blue

AT DAYBREAK on a summer morning in 1784 young Sam Dale and his small brother watched from their hiding place as two Negro slaves named Mose and Lum swung open the heavy gates of Carmichael's Fort. Then Sam pulled his brother's hand and the two boys slipped out of the gate behind the cattle being herded into the newly gathered corn field. They were not quite quick enough. Mose's big black hand descended onto Sam's shoulder.

"You boys got no bizness outside dis heah fort!" he said sternly. "Yo' paw would skin you alive if'n he ketched you outside dese gates."

"Aw, Mose, don't tell on us, please," wheedled Sam with a mischievous gleam in his blue eyes that was hard to resist. "Alex and me have been waitin' since befo' daybreak to go coon huntin'. We had to sneak out befo' anybody woke up. Anyway," he grinned, "you know there hasn't been a sign of Injuns all summer or you wouldn't be wearin' that fine blue coat!"

Mose glanced down at the shining gold buttons on the long-tailed robin's egg blue coat that was his most treasured possession. It had come all the way from Virginia and had been given to him by his master Mr. Carmichael for saving his life during an Indian attack in the Spring. Mose had caught a sideways glimpse of an Indian rifle barrel and had flung the old man down into the dust in the split second before the bullet whizzed past. Since then Mose and the blue coat had seldom been parted.

Now Mose turned to his partner. "What d'you think, Lum," he asked. "Reckon it'll be awright?"

Lum scratched his head. "Dey be good boys in de woods," he nodded slowly. "Dey paw's brung 'em up to be keerfiil."

Mose still seemed doubtful, and Sam looked longingly toward the woods where the dawn mist was already beginning to disperse as the gray sky grew brighter. "Tell you what, Mose," Sam pleaded. "If we ketch a coon, we will give him to you and Lum. I just want the fun of treein' him. And we will be careful, I promise!" He looked very eager and confident, broad-shouldered and tall for his eleven years, with a square chin and a straightforward look in his eyes. Nine year old Alex worshipped Sam and always followed his brother's lead. Finally Mose nodded reluctantly and turned back to the milling cattle as the boys scampered away.

Sam Dale had been brought to the restless Georgia frontier when he was only eight years old and had been coached in all the lore of the woods by his father. He had already acquired the skilled woodsman's soft-footed way of walking and was as alert and graceful as a young animal. Today Sam had a special reason for feeling confident. Hidden under his fringed buckskin hunting shirt was an old holster pistol loaded with buckshot.

Pa had given it to him after that scary night last April when a band of Creeks had slipped inside the stockade and had set fire to the high pile of corn shucks piled up against the storehouse. Sam and Alex had managed to sneak outside under cover of Pa and Ma's rifle shots. They had run to the corn pen, pulled down the rails, and let the high pile of corn slip down on the blazing shucks, which soon smothered the flames.

There were so few people in the fort at the time that Pa had made all the women dress up in overcoats and hats to look like men.

The trick had fooled the Indians and they had left. Soon afterwards Pa had given Sam the old pistol and showed him how to use it.

Soon after they entered the woods, Alex spotted a coon. His eyes danced with excitement as he touched Sam's arm and silently pointed. From then on the little ring-tailed creature led them on a merry chase as it scampered under bushes and briars. Finally the two sweating and exhausted boys converged on their prey and managed to chase it into a tall hickory tree. Sam tried to boost the smaller boy up to the nearest limb, but it was no use. "It's too far," Alex said sadly. "Maybe if you stood on my shoulders."

"I'd squash you like a bug," laughed Sam, looking at Alex's skinny legs.

"No, you won't," Alex protested manfully. "I'll brace my back against the tree like this." He squared his thin shoulders and held himself rigid under Sam's moccasined foot as the older boy managed to scramble up to the lowest branch. From there it was an easy climb to the swaying top where the 'coon was clinging. With a smile of triumph Sam reached out his hand to shake the limb. The boys were so absorbed that they barely heard the first distant rifle shot. But with the second shot Sam jerked to awareness and his spine tingled. "Run, Alex, run!" he mouthed in a hoarse whisper. "Tell the fort! Quick! Vamoose!"

As Alex obediently sped away, Sam took stock of his own position. He had descended only a few limbs when a bloodcurdling scream froze his blood. With his arms clinging to the great trunk of the tree, he cautiously peered through the leafy branches. About a hundred yards off, Lum came staggering out of a thicket with Mose racing beside him, the skirts of his long-tailed blue coat flying out behind him as he fled. Chasing him were three Creek Indians.

When they got to the hickory, the Indian seized the tails of Mose's coat but they tore off under his grasp. He next seized the collar and jerked at it, tearing the coat off Mose's back, but in the effort the Indian fell and dropped his rifle. That was all that saved the black man's life. Mose put on a fresh burst of speed and headed for home.

Meanwhile the other two Indians had finished their gory task of scalping poor Lum and were standing under Sam's tree. They appeared to be armed only with tomahawks. Sam wondered if he dared to use the old pistol. Before he could give himself time to be afraid, he had leveled the weapon and fired, killing one of the Indians. The other bolted away, but by this time the third Indian had returned from chasing Mose and was leaning over to pick up his rifle.

Sam knew that whatever he did now had better be done in a hurry. Suddenly he began to get a glimmer of an idea. His father had taught him to be a keen observer of the animals of the forest. Sam had often been baffled for hours by a fox squirrel in a tree who would watch Sam's motions and go round and round so as to keep the trunk of the tree between them.

Now Sam played this game with the Indian. Every time the Indian brought the rifle up to shoot, Sam would duck behind the tree. The Indian fired twice, barking the tree close to Sam's ears. Sam knew his arms could not hold out much longer.

Just as the Indian raised the rifle for a third try, Sam's ringing ears caught the sound of galloping hoofs. Mose's strong arms caught him as he toppled from the tree. By the time the victorious rescuers came back from dispatching the last of the raiding Indians, Sam was able to hold himself proudly erect. He drew a deep breath into his quivering lungs and looked in dazed wonder at the copper-colored body stretched at his feet. He had killed his first Indian.

"There's just one thing, Pa," said Sam as he rode behind his father toward the fort. "I'm sad about Mose's fine blue coat. It's tore all to pieces and he was so proud of it."

Sam's father talked it over with old Mr. Carmichael and the

other men, and they all felt the same. It was sad enough that Mose's friend Lum had been killed. Losing his coat on top of that seemed to take away half the big man's glory. But what could they do?

Finally somebody remembered an old bedridden Revolutionary War veteran who lived over in the Holston settlements. Maybe he had something he would sell them. Sam and Alex eagerly collected subscriptions, and there was not a single one of the thirty families in the fort who failed to contribute.

When the time came around for Mose to fiddle for the next hoedown on Saturday night, he was a sight to dazzle the eyes, his big frame encased in a splendid long-tailed coat with gold buttons and epaulets. He proudly wore the dress uniform of a full colonel of militia in the Georgia Volunteers.

Historical Notes on "Sam Dale and the Long-tailed Blue"

The Long-tail Blue: *Life and Times of Sam Dale,* J.F.H. Claiborne, Harpers, N.Y., 1860

The main events of the story were related to Claiborne by Sam Dale. Claiborne was his personal friend as well as his biographer.

—Sam Dale: from Claiborne's biography. Sam's mother and father, of Scotch-Irish descent, were natives of Pennsylvania who moved to Virginia when Sam was three, and later moved to Georgia where they took refuge from the Creeks in Carmichael's Station.

When Sam Dale was seventeen his mother died in childbirth with her ninth child and his heartbroken father died a week later. Sam then took responsibility for his orphaned brothers and his sister Jane. Within two years he had paid off his father's debts and was earning wages as a scout for the United States Army. Later he was commissioned as a brigadier-general by the Alabama Legislature. Dale County and numerous towns are named for him.

—The Canoe Fight and the Ride to New Orleans: Dale's best known exploit was the Canoe Fight on the Alabama River, where he and two companions battled and defeated eleven Indians in a war canoe while a Negro named Caesar held the canoes together.

Equally well known was his 700-mile ride to New Orleans with dispatches from Washington, D.C., for General Andrew Jackson. He made the ride on his pony Paddy in eight days, in time to witness the Battle of New Orleans, then rode Paddy back to Georgia in eight days, bringing news of the successful battle which helped Jackson become the President of the United States.

The Dance of Death

TOM JAMES, a towheaded and freckled boy of fourteen, jerked upright from his straw pallet in the grip of a nightmare. All around him in Fort Sinquefield refugees from the Indian fighting lay sleeping. Tom peered into the darkness, but only the drowsy sentries or the occasional wail of a sleepy baby broke the stillness of the hot September night. Suddenly Tom realized that the nightmare that had awakened him had really happened that very morning. He knew that the horrible scenes of blood and destruction printed behind his eyeballs would never go away.

He and his older sister Mary would probably be dead, too, if Isham Kimball had not persuaded them to go fishing that morning. They'd had a great time splashing along the creek except that he was disgusted at the way Mary kept flirting with Isham, pretending to lose her balance on the stepping stones and then leaning on him for support, tossing her curls and looking up at him from under her eyelashes. It was just the way their sister Sarah had flirted before she married Jack Merrill, and now the Merrills had a year-old baby, though Sarah was just eighteen. Mary used to be fun, he thought, just like another boy.

It was late morning as they were coming home that the horror began. That was when Tom saw the moccasin track. It was fresh and it pointed downstream. "'Twasn't there this morning," Tom had whispered, and Isham had nodded. Then they had caught the first smell, a vagrant whiff of woodsmoke mingled with burnt flesh that brought with it a sick feeling of nausea and panic. Tom shuddered, remembering. The next events flashed across his mind in a series of vivid pictures.

He saw himself creeping up on the burned cabin while Isham stayed behind to protect Mary. He saw again the grotesque litter of bodies and relived his horror as he recognized the blackened hulk sprawled across the door sill as Mrs. Kimball, Isham's mother, her big arms spread across the corpses of the two youngest children. The bodies of Abel and Jim, Isham's small brothers, lay under the big oak where they had their tree house. They had been shot full of arrows and their heads bashed in with clubs. Tom could read the story of how the three little girls had died from the grisly remains on the log palings of the garden fence. The Indians must have picked them up by the feet and dashed their heads against the wall, for they lay in a row where they had fallen.

Sarah's body lay just beyond them, looking so lifelike that Tom thought at first she might be only unconscious. He reached out to touch her. Then he saw the great wound on her scalp and the pool of blood and jerked his hand away. He felt a stab of pity for her husband, Jack Merrill, off fighting somewhere and not even knowing.

Then suddenly he had heard a faint sound, almost like a groan. Then it came again, from over behind the well coping. Now Tom could see two feathered arrows sticking up at a crazy angle. The arrows moved, and he recognized his father's buckskin hunting jacket. Abner James must have fallen and knocked himself out on that rock, Tom decided, as he vainly tried to raise his father's stocky body. A good thing Pa was bald-headed, he thought with grim humor, or he'd have been scalped like the others.

The rest of that long terrible day was all jumbled up together in his mind, how he and Isham had struggled to support Pa on the four-mile walk to the fort, with Mary sobbing all the way. Finally, though, Isham had got Mary calmed down enough to tear pieces off her skirt to bind up Pa's wounds. By they time they reached Fort Sinquefield Abner had recovered enough to tell his story.

"I'd gone to the shed for stovewood," he told them. "Reckon that's how come they never seen me. Somethin' made me look up and there they were, more'n thirty of 'em, all naked and painted black, creepin' upon the house in a circle. Remember when Sam Dale told us about hidin' and watchin' them Shawnees do the dance of the lakes?"

Tom remembered every detail that big Sam Dale had told them of how the naked, black-painted prophets, as they called themselves, had danced silently in single file before the Indian chiefs gathered to hear Tecumseh. They had brandished their war clubs, he said, and jerked all over, with buffalo tails hanging from their arms and waistbands, and eagle plumes on their heads. It was called the Dance of Death. Tom even remembered some of the words of Tecumseh's speech that Sam Dale had overheard as he lay hidden in the forest. "Drive the Pale Faces back upon a trail of blood," Tecumseh had shouted. "Burn their dwellings! Slay their wives and children! . . . This is the will of the Great Spirit, revealed to my brother, the Prophet."

Just last week Pa had been warned that Tecumseh's half-breed brother, Josiah Francis, the Prophet, was ravaging the Forks country with his black-painted followers who called themselves prophets. Sam Dale had urged the settlers not to leave the protection of the fort, and Tom knew they had been wrong to leave. But Mrs. Kimball, who had kept house for them since his mother died, had nagged at Abner James night and day about the scanty provisions in the fort, the stink and the filth, with the six little ones always getting underfoot and half of them sick. That was what had finally changed Abner's mind.

"It's the muddy water in this old shallow well that keeps 'em ailin'," Mrs. Kimball insisted, pursing her fat cheeks. "I keep thinkin' of that fine freestone well back at the home place."

So they had left the fort, and now Abner was feeling guilty and grieving for the dead children. Mary had begun sobbing again. "I hate this country," she had moaned. "I want to go back to Georgia where it's safe. Nothin's going to keep me here, either, not you or anybody else!" She had jerked her arm away from Isham's grasp and stalked ahead of him, her eyes on the ground.

"Giver her time, boy," Abner had muttered. "It's worst on the women, God knows!"

That night as they walked toward their rough shed, Tom said to Isham, "I'm kinda worried about Pa." He looked towards where Abner rested on a pile of moldy straw, his face gray with fatigue and his eyes staring into space.

"Yeah, he's taking it pretty hard," answered Isham. "The colonel tried to make him lay down a while, but he didn't even answer, just picked up his gun and started back to his place on the wall."

Mary was coming toward them with a platter of beans and stale bread and a steaming kettle. "Tain't real coffee, just sweet potato brew." She shook her father's shoulder in an effort to rouse him from his dark mood. "C'mon, Pa, you've got to eat," she pleaded.

Tom thought how different Mary looked from yesterday morning when they were playing in the creek. Her hair was pulled back in a hasty plait, and her mouth was set in a tight line as if she had forgotten how to smile. Isham might as well not have been there, for Mary didn't even notice him. She was watching Mrs. Phillips, who was obviously pregnant, and suddenly she burst out, "How could any woman want to bring a baby into something like this!" Her angry, accusing glance swept past them over the noise and confusion of the fort — the screaming children and barking dogs, the tired defenders and worried women. They had no answer.

Tom looked up to see the tall figure of Colonel Carson striding toward the shed. "Oh, here you are," he rumbled as he squatted down beside Abner. "Just the folks I wanted to see." Then he hesitated in obvious embarrassment. "I don't know if I should tell you this — you've so much to worry you — but I guess I don't have the right to keep it from you."

Abner looked up in alarm and the colonel added hastily, "It isn't bad news exactly. It's just, well, my men couldn't find the bodies of Sarah and her baby. We don't know yet what it means. The Indians could have carried 'em off, of course." He turned to Tom. "You did see her there with the others?"

"I did, sir," Tom stated positively. "At first I thought she looked alive, but then I saw they'd scalped her."

Mary gasped and burst out sobbing, but Tom had a sudden stirring of hope, though he dared not speak his thoughts aloud. On the way into the Forks country he had talked with an old man at a tavern who had been scalped and had the scars to prove it. So it could happen. Before he fell asleep that night on his straw pallet, Tom said a silent prayer for Sarah and her baby.

Next morning the guards jabbered excitedly at the approaching sound of a hard-ridden horse. Tom heard someone call out, "It's Jere Austell! I'd know him anywhere!" Others yelled, "He's got someone with him. Looks like a woman," and then, "By gum! Hit's a woman an' a baby!"

By the time Tom had pushed through the crowd, his heart pounding with a wild hope, they had laid the woman on a quilt. Then he was outside and he could see. It was Sarah. She had ridden tied on behind Austell, half-fainting and with a bloody rag wrapped around her head. But she was alive and the baby, too!

Gentle hands tended the injured girl while Granny Potter hurried to fetch salves and bandages. Now Mary had come up and was reaching for the baby boy. Tom watched Mary's face soften above the baby in her arms. It seemed a long time since he'd seen Mary smile like that. Then Pa was there, and he saw with surprise that tears were rolling down Pa's cheeks. It was the first time Tom had ever seen a man cry, but he felt sort of like crying himself.

Later, young Jere Austell told them what he had learned from Sarah, who was now asleep. "I was ridin' at night, bein' plenty careful, as you kin imagine, when I smelled the burnt-out cabin and come on Injun sign about the yard. I cut offn' the trail in case the varmints wuz still around, an' I hadn't rid far before I heard a moanin' sound. Then I come up on this pore girl. How she got that far I'll never know! Seems she'd come to her senses when it started to rain. Then she'd heard her baby cry and managed to crawl over to him.

"They'd thrown him against a wall and stunned him but he wasn't hurt too bad and he didn't have hair enough to scalp. Well, she'd bound up her scalped head with pieces of her petticoat and carried the baby off as far as she could. When he got too heavy, she hid him behind a hollow log and went on by herself. When I come up on her she was about gone, but she managed to tell me about the baby afore she fainted. I tell you, folks, that's a brave girl!"

Under the watchful care of Granny Potter and the women, Sarah's wound began to heal. Luckily the knife had not gone deep enough to injure her brain. There had been one last outburst from Mary when Sam Dale had come over to help them defend the fort and had offered to conduct anyone to more settled country who did not wish to stay. "I don't want to stay here," Mary had shouted. "I hate Indians, the mean, sneaky varmints! I never want to see another one!"

"I understand how you feel," Sam said gently, sitting down and putting his buckskin-clad arm around her. "The Indians do some savage things when they're stirred up and scared of being pushed out of their land. But they aren't all bad. Half the people massacred at Fort Mims were Indians or half-breeds, killed because they were friendly to whites!"

Mary and Tom looked at him in wonder.

Sam Dale smiled sadly. "You didn't know that? Why, I wouldn't be here tonight if a brave Indian woman hadn't saved my life last week. She warned me of a planned attack on me by hostile Indians along the Wolf Path."

Then Sarah had spoken up from where she sat with her baby. She was still pale and weak but was slowly regaining her strength. "It's not safe anywhere," she said now, "but I feel safer being here with you than goin' off among strangers. Maybe pretty soon I'll be able to shoot a gun!"

Mary went over to Sarah then and hugged her, and no more was said about leaving. Tom looked around the circle of faces as he spooned up his bowl of cornbread mush. The glow of the torches lit up Sam Dale's high cheekbones and big crooked nose and firm chin as he talked about the defense of the fort.

It was strange, Tom thought, how homelike this place seemed to him now. Pa had come out of his shell and was talking about the best way of molding bullets. Then Tom looked over at Mary. She was holding hands with Isham and looking up at him from under her eyelashes. He gave a long sigh. That's a girl for you, he thought, always flirting.

Historical Notes on "The Dance of Death"

Sam Dale: (from J.F.H. Claiborne's *Life and Times of General Sam Dale*, Harpers, N.Y., 1860

General Claiborne, who fought beside Sam Dale in the Creek War, wrote this biography mostly in Dale's own words. In it Dale described his early life on the Georgia frontier and tells of hiding in the woods to hear Tecumseh's speech and to watch the "dance of the lakes" by the Shawnee prophets. Dale also told how Bob Mosely's Indian wife, the niece of Peter McQueen of the Red Sticks, saved his life by her timely warning.

Josiah Francis and the Prophets: (from A.J. Pickett's *History of Alabama*, 1850; repub. NewSouth Books, Montgomery, 2001)

"Josiah Francis was the son of a Creek woman and a Scotch trader . . . Francis won many other subordinate prophets. He also introduced the practice of jerking and trembling all over, used incantations, and claimed to be instructed by the Great Spirit. He led the Alabamos against other Indians friendly to whites."

The Abner James and Ransom Kemball Families: (from Pickett's *History of Alabama*, see above)

"Abner James and Ransom Kemball with their large families, being inmates of Fort Sinquefield and dissatisfied at its crowded conditions, repaired to Kemball's house two miles from the fort. Here they were when Josiah Francis surrounded the house. Abner James, his fourteen year old son Thomas, and his daughter Mary escaped and fled to the fort. Isham Kemball, sixteen, also got safely away (he later became clerk of Circuit Court of Clark Co.) All the others were killed by war clubs and scalped.

"In the early evening a slight rain began which revived Sarah Merrill, Abner James' married daughter. She felt among the bodies and found her twelve-months-old boy alive and breast fed him. She then got to her feet and walked with him toward the fort, though she had been severely beaten and the top of her head scalped. The baby had been slung against the house and cut on the head, but his hair was too short to scalp."

Colonel Carson and the Burial at Fort Sinquefield: *(Pickett's History of Alabama,* see above)

"Colonel Carson went with seven dragoons and three spies to bury the dead. They brought twelve bodies to Fort Sinquefield in an oxcart to throw into a pit dug fifty yards from the gate. The whole garrison attended the simple ceremony."

Jeremiah Austill: (from Caldwell Delaney's Graighead's *Mobile,* The Haunted Bookshop, Mobile, 1968)

"Jeremiah Austill, merchant and farmer, 19, riding alone at night through hostile country to relieve Fort Stephens, came on 'signs' of Indians — a burned house and bodies — rode further into the woods where he heard moans and found a scalped woman left to die. He tied the woman to his horse, found her baby son hidden in a hollow log, and carried the baby in his arms to Fort Sinquefield."

What Happened Years Later; (from *Montgomery Advertiser;* "Alabama Pioneer Scalped but Lived," by Ed Williams, June 15, 1976)

"When Gordon Anderson of Grove Hill was a child, his grandmother — whose grandmother was Sarah Merrill — often told him the story of how Sarah was scalped and survived. Mrs. Merrill's husband was with Gen. Claiborne at the Battle of Horseshoe Bend."

The Whipping

JUST AFTER the first rooster crowed, a small dark figure slipped silently out of the darker shadow of a Negro cabin in the potato field behind the sleeping fort. Gif knew he bad to hurry to get down to the shore of Tensaw Lake before daybreak. This was the only time he had to himself. All day long he had to carry water and cut firewood for the refugees sheltered in the fort, with more of them coming in every day. But his first job was to take care of Miss Ellie. Especially now, with the baby ailing and her so worried looking.

Gif had his work for this morning all planned out. Now he fingered the knife in his pocket, glad he'd put a good sharp edge on it the night before. He wished he had some gloves, though. Those water reeds would be tough. He remembered cutting his hands on them when he used to help his mother make baskets back home before she died of swamp sickness. Now it looked to him like Miss Ellie's baby, little Howie, was getting the same kind of fever. Gif shivered in the cold February wind from off the lake and hurried toward the shelter of the tall canes, careful to start cutting his reeds a safe distance above the pickets posted down by the old Boat Yard.

His agile brown fingers had not forgotten their skill, and by daylight Gif had made a good start. As he worked, he pictured how the baby-carrying basket would look strapped to Miss Ellie's back.

He'd gotten the idea from the ones he'd seen the Indian women use on Miss Sophia's plantation upriver where he had been raised.

It seemed strange to think of Miss Sophia being half-Indian herself, since she was such a fine great lady now. But her brother, General Alexander McGillivray, who had owned Gif's grandfather, had been the greatest chief in the whole Creek Nation.

Gif still felt homesick whenever he thought about Miss Sophia. She had taken him into the big house when his mother had died and taught him how to help with the household chores. Sometimes she had told stories to the children about her early life among the Indians on the Alabama River where Alexander's plantation was. As she talked of those days her eyes would shine with excitement, and the lines in her face would smooth out so that Gif could imagine how beautiful she must have been when she was young. He wished he were back there now. He hated this crowded fort, but he knew Miss Sophia was counting on him.

When she had given him to the young Halls as a wedding present, Miss Sophia had made him promise to take good care of them. That had been last year when he was going on fifteen, but the way Miss Sophia put it had made him feel like a grown man with a real job to do.

"Miss Ellie's so young and not real strong," she had said, "and I'm not sure how well Howard can manage off by himself like that and starting from scratch. I've watched how you took charge of your sick grandfather, and now that he's gone, you need a family to look after and those two could surely use some help!"

It had worked out real good, too, right from the start. Mr. Howard had grinned when Gif told him his name was Aloysius. "I'll never be able to wrap my tongue around that name," he laughed. "What'll we call him, Ellie?"

Miss Ellie had thought about it, with her yellow head on one side and a twinkle in her blue eyes. "Well," she'd smiled, "he's our best wedding gift, thanks to Aunt Sophia, so why don't we just call him Gift?"

That suited Gif just fine. He'd thought he was going to be stuck with Aloysius for life. Everything had been going along just fine until the Indian raids had started up and they had come down the river to this place. Morning sounds were coming from the fort now — hungry babies crying, new sentries marching out, horses whinnying. The smell of bacon and coffee drifted down from early campfires.

My belly sure feels empty, thought Gif as he turned to gather up his reeds. Suddenly his hands froze in mid air. Was that a faint rustle behind him in the dry cane stalks? His keen eyes searched the brown mud at his feet. Was it a snake? No, it was not that kind of sound. Not like a small animal would make, but something bigger. Indians? Gif rolled his eyes cautiously sideways without turning his head. Then he let out a sigh of relief. The face peering out from between the cane stalks was as black as his own.

"C'mon out, man! You skeered me half to death," Gif said softly. "Ain' nobody goin' to hurt you."

The crouched figure unfolded itself from the canes to tower above him, and now Gif could see that the ragged homespun clothes were crusted with dried blood. "I'm Joe, fum Mr. McGrath's place upriver at Claiborne," the man told him. "I wuz feered them sojers would shoot fust an' ask questions later. Lawd, that food sho smells good! I bin on de trail a week an' ain't et fer two days!"

"You kin have some of me an' Jumbo's rations up to our cabin," said Gif, leading the way across the field, "an' then we kin talk. You look like you bin clawed by a bear!"

It had not been a bear he had tangled with but a band of Creek Indians, Joe told the two boys after he had taken the edge off his hunger with their leftover cow peas and fatback. Joe and three other McGrath hands had been kidnapped by the Indians while they were out looking for stray cattle. They had beaten Joe half to death trying to get him to tell how many soldiers had gone down river to help the settlers at the fort.

"I didn't tell 'em nothin'," claimed Joe, "but they got it out of one of de others, so when I got a chance to slip off, I figgered I'd bettah git down here an' give de warnin'. I know a little of dere Muskogee talk, an' fum whut I gathered they wuz plannin' to meet a bigger bunch of Injuns at the Cutoff an' all of 'em is headed dis way!"

After Joe told his story, he pulled off his tattered shirt to show a back crisscrossed with deep gashes made by a rawhide whip. It was a pitiful sight. Gif had heard of masters who whipped their people. Jumbo had told him how his own master, Mr. John Randon, had given him a licking once just because he was lazy and a slow poke.

As Gif gently bathed Joe's half-healed cuts in warm water and bound them up with clean sacking, he thought again how lucky he was to belong to the young Halls. They had built him a snug little shed room off the kitchen of their new cabin and Miss Ellie had fed him the same food she fixed for her husband. It seemed like months instead of two weeks since they had come to this miserable crowded fort, and now things looked worse than ever, with painted Indians about to sneak up on them. Jumbo was a strong, good-natured fellow, but he didn't have much sense, so Gif figured the next move was up to him.

"We bes' take him to the major right off," he decided. "Joe's traveled a fur piece to bring him de warnin'."

A short time later the exhausted Joe, flanked by the two boys, was led toward the plank table where Major Beasley and his officers were having breakfast. Joe's story caused an uproar, as Gif had expected, and soon the major was bellowing out orders and everybody was rushing around like a bunch of chickens when a fox came around. In the confusion Gif slipped off to see about Miss Ellie and the baby.

The Halls had been among the first arrivals at the unfinished stockade, so they'd had the pick of the board sheds at the rear of the clapboard farmhouse. Gif was proud of the way he had arranged things to make them comfortable. But that was before the Randons had moved in with them. The old couple and their daughter Miss Elouisa, who had married Miss Sophia's rich nephew David Tate, had brought all sorts of fine fixings and fancy food from Pensacola. It took some of the shine off the times when Gif had managed to snare a rabbit or to bring in a string of fresh caught fish from the lake.

But the worst thing, to Gif's way of thinking, was the way Miss Elouisa took charge of everything, especially the baby. Maybe it was because she missed her own little girl who had been left with her Aunt Sophia upriver. Miss Ellie's baby still looked peaked, though, in spite of that woman always fussing over him.

Old Miz Randon wasn't so bad. She was a big, soft Indian woman — mostly she was talking or eating — but Miss Elouisa and Mr. John Randon were cold people, hard-mouthed and purse-proud, trying to make out like they were better than ordinary folks.

They'd acted shocked when they found Gif making up his bed nearby, in case he could help out during the night with the sick baby, and had ordered him to sleep with Jumbo in one of the shacks outside the palings. Gif had thought there for a minute that Mr. Howard was going to speak up for him, but Mr. Howard had been brought up to be respectful to his elders, and it was easy to see that Mr. John Randon wasn't used to being talked back to. So Mr. Howard hadn't said anything — only, just as Gif had ducked his head to go outside, he'd given him a wink to let him know how he felt.

When the excitement in the fort over Joe's warning had quieted down a little, Major Beasley sent out a bunch of soldiers under the youngest Randon boy, Peter, with Joe to guide them back to where the Indians had held him captive. While they were gone, Gif noticed there was more defense work done than in the whole time since they'd been in the fort. Some of the men even gave up their jawing and gambling and wrestling contests long enough to work on the unfinished blockhouse in the raised southeast corner of the log wall. But when the scouting party returned a few days later without having seen hide nor hair of Indians, it seemed like things drifted into worse shape than ever.

Maybe it was because they'd all been cooped up together so long. Some folks' supplies were running low, and they got to bickering with those that had more, calling them stingy when they wouldn't share. Everybody was edgy and the nights were real spooky. Whatever was the reason, the talk started going around that Joe was just a runaway who had made up the whole story. Old Mr. Randon had talked himself into this way of thinking and once his mind was set, there wasn't any changing it.

As Gif stood in the line at the well with his empty water buckets, he could hear old Mr. Randon's harsh voice rising angrily from the group of men clustered around him. "I'm convinced that nigger's lying," he was proclaiming, "as I've said all along. My son Peter here will back me on it that they found nary a sign of Indians. Ain't that right, son?"

But Gif noticed that Peter took his time answering. He was the only one of the three Randon boys that was not cowed by his father.

Peter was popular with the men of the fort and had been chosen as one of their two captains because he had fought so well last summer at the battle of Burnt Corn. Now he drawled thoughtfully, "Well, Paw, you can't say for sure there wasn't no Indians jus' because we didn't see none! We made as much noise in the woods as a herd of buffalo, an' I kep' feelin' like they was hidin' out there an' watchin' us."

Old Mr. Ranson wasn't even listening, thought Gif, and now it looked like he was going to make trouble for poor Joe. "Well, I say a good whipping would soon have the truth out of him," his stern voice came again. "I suggest some of us speak to Major Beasley about it."

Some of the men were nodding their heads, and their voices got lower. Gif's thoughts were racing now. As soon as he got his chores done, he'd better get word to Joe to high-tail it out of this place before those men gave him a worse licking than the Indians had. The Randons had brought so much food they wouldn't miss it if he fixed up a parcel for Joe while they were eating lunch. And Gif had spotted an old piece of a rowboat down in the reeds. It probably wouldn't hold together long, but it might give Joe a start.

Next morning when the major's duly appointed committee found that their quarry had disappeared, John Randon took it for proof that he'd been right and Joe's whole story had been made up to cover his being a runaway. The older Randon sons backed him up, but Peter and some of the younger men weren't so sure. They kept going out on scouting parties, and one of the men thought he saw some Indian sign. But after a week dragged by with nothing happening, folks began to relax.

Gif might have felt a little easier, though he believed Joe's story, if he hadn't happened to overhear Miss Elouisa arguing with her husband, Mr. David. Gif admired Mr. David Tate more than any man he knew, and so did most everybody else. Many a time Miss Sophia or Gif's grandfather had told him of how David Tate, when he was only twelve, had traveled to New York with his uncle, General Alexander McGillivray, and had been sent to school up north for four years by President George Washington himself. Then he had finished College in Scotland.

David Tate could have had a high position among the Yankees, but instead he'd chosen to come back to his own Creek Indian people when General Alexander McGillivray died. Gif had seen Mr. David's fine plantation at Montpelier and his big herds of cattle, but sometimes he wondered whether Mr. David was ever sorry he'd comeback south, now that his own half-brother, the one they called Red Eagle, was on the warpath. Mr. David's family were not the only relatives Red Eagle was fighting. The fort was just full of Miss Sophia's kinfolks.

Gif hadn't meant to eavesdrop on Mr. David and his wife. He'd finished work for the day and had dropped down on the grass to rest a moment outside the back gate. He had leaned his tired back against the log wall and was watching the last of the sunset and thinking how peaceful it was when he heard them.

He couldn't mistake Mr. David's nice sounding way of talking — folks always took notice when Mr. David spoke — and it was just as easy to recognize Miss Elouisa's clipped-off way of talking. When he looked up, Gif realized why he could hear so plainly. They must be standing right next to one of the portholes that had been cut into the log wall every few feet.

"For the last time, Lou," Mr. David was saying, "I wish you'd come with me to Pierce's place." His voice was low and serious, and Gif couldn't move away for wondering what was coming next. After all, he had his own folks to think about. Now Miss Elouisa was talking.

"With Pa and the boys and a whole company of soldiers here, why should you expect me to go trekking off to an unprotected farmhouse three miles away?"

"Pierce is an old man and a neutral," Mr. David told her. "I talked to my brother William there tonight secretly, hoping to move him to see reason. It's true he's ordered his men to respect women and children, but I'm not at all sure he can control them once the fighting begins — and it's coming, Lou, and soon, in spite of all my efforts."

"How can William fight his own kin?" Miss Elouisa was asking. "I can't understand him!"

"I think he sees himself as a savior of his people. He gets carried away with his own words," Mr. David answered slowly as if he were thinking it out. "Although William has more white blood in him than I do, he's actually all Indian. He refused an education — said the forest was the only world he ever wanted. He thinks he can make the Creeks a great nation again as Alexander McGillivray did. But he was too young to understand our uncle as I did. The secret of Alexander's power was that he constantly maneuvered to keep the peace. He knew that if we fought the white man we would be destroyed."

The voices sank to a murmur now. They were saying good-bye. Gif walked slowly toward his cabin. He had a lot to think about. In the morning he would have his carrying basket finished except for the lining. For that he would need to boil some Spanish moss to kill the bugs in it, and then dry it in the sun. He had already put aside some meal sacks to make the padding. It looked more than ever like they might need that basket in a hurry.

The next morning was sunny and mild with a feel of Spring in the air. Gif thought of his moss drying on the grass and wondered if he could finish the lining after they brought the cows in. He was glad it was his and Jumbo's turn to be cowherds on such a fine day. Jumbo never talked much, and it was nice and quiet in the meadow across from the fort. Some children ran out of the propped-open gate chasing a ball, and he could hear a woman's voice calling them back, but it sounded faint and far away like another world.

A breeze stirred, and Gif thought he smelled a whiff of that pink honeysuckle that some folks called wild azaleas. It was too early in the year, but there might be some in bloom down in the ravine where they could get their roots in water. Gif glanced through the screen of blackjack oaks at the edge of the ravine and thought he saw a flash of pink way down at the bottom.

As he peered more closely, his sharp eyes caught a flicker of movement. Fear clutched his stomach. Beyond the pink bloom was a streak of vermilion war paint on a brown face. Gif steeled himself not to move a single muscle. He had to be sure. Now that he knew they were there, he spotted another and another. He mustn't let them know they had been seen. Carefully he rolled over on his back and lay there until his heart stopped pounding.

When he got to his feet, his legs were trembling, but he made himself walk slowly toward Jumbo. "C'mon, less go get somethin' to eat," he said casually.

Jumbo was always ready to eat, but he knew it wasn't time yet. "Mistah Randon, he'll give me what-for, do I come in dis early," he protested.

Gif just said "C'mon" again and walked off.

Jumbo kept pestering him all the way across the meadow, but Gif wouldn't say another word until they were at the open gate. Then he breathed softly, "That gully was full of Indians! I dasn't tell you fer fear you'd start hollerin' an' mebbe git us kilt!"

He'd sure sized Jumbo up right, Gif thought disgustedly. There Jumbo went, staggering up to Mr. Randon and gobbling like a turkey.

Here came Mr. Randon's cronies gathering around to ask him questions. Gif saw Mr. Randon coming and hurried off toward his young master before anyone could stop him.

"It's true, Mr. Howard!" he gasped. "Jumbo didn't see the Injuns, but I did, down in the gully. I looked real close an' counted three for sure, maybe more. I didn' let on 'cause I had to git back to let you an' Miss Ellie know!" To Gif's horror he felt tears come into his eyes.

Mr. Howard put a hand on his shoulder. "Thank you, Gif," he said softly.

But here came old Mr. Randon, puffed up and mad-looking. "Howard, from all I can get out of this idiot boy of mine, he didn't see a thing! It's yore nigger that's dreamed up this whole cock and bull story. They will see ha'nts behind ev'ry bush if it'll get 'em out of a day's work!" He gave a grim chuckle. "I'm going to give my boy a whippin' he won't soon forget for scarin' all these good ladies, and I'd suggest you do the same."

Gif would never forget what happened next. He hadn't seen Miss Ellie come up, but she'd heard it all. She didn't say a word, but she stepped right up beside Mr. Howard and put her arm through his and looked up into his face. Mr. Howard never even took his arm off Gif's shoulder, and he spoke right up to Mr. Randon, real quiet but firm, too. "What you do, sir, is your own concern. But I trust this boy of mine, and I won't have him whipped."

Then he and Miss Ellie turned and walked off toward their shed, pushing Gif along in front of them. Miss Sophia would sure have been proud of them.

As soon as he could speak without being overheard, Gif told Miss Ellie he had something to give her, but it was down at his cabin. "Whilst I run git it, you'd best be packin' us up some food while them Randons is watchin' pore ol' Jumbo git his whippin'!"

Miss Ellie looked a question at Mr. Howard, and he nodded his head. Gif was already racing toward the back gate. It was propped open like the front gate and nobody was watching it. Everybody was watching Jumbo and listening to him holler. In a few minutes Gif was back with his basket. Miss Ellie was real pleased when she saw how it worked. Gif had made straps for it out of an old piece of harness.

"'Course I made it fer the baby," said Gif, "but while we got the chance, we kin put our supplies in it an' I'll go hide 'em in my cabin till it's dark enough fer us to slip off."

Miss Ellie didn't waste any time, and the two packs were quickly made up with a three days' supply of food. They would take turns carrying little Howie.

"I'll nurse the baby the last thing before we leave so he'll be quiet and sleepy," Miss Ellie said. "Then we'll just walk out for a breath of air — and never come back, and then we'll be a family again." She sighed. "I'll be glad to get shed of the Randons!"

But as things turned out, they weren't through with the Randons after all. At first everything went off as smooth as silk. They had got safely away from the fort and were in the first stand of trees when a man's figure moved quietly from behind a pine tree. Gif's heart sank, but the man had a hand to his mouth to shush them, and then Gif could make out the tall figure of Peter Randon.

"I ain't goin' to give you away — jus' come to wish you luck," he whispered. "Pa's been doin' some wishful thinkin', and he's wrong! I'm takin' my own bunch out to hunt around till we find them sneakin' Red Stick varmints."

After Peter gave them some advice about the best way to go, he slipped back into the woods. Now it was many weary hours later, and they were trudging off across the plains toward the east. Mr. Howard and Peter Randon had helped Mr. David Tate drive some of his cattle to market over that way, so there would be a sort of halfway trail. They'd walk all night and hide in the swamps during the daytime.

Gif was thinking as he walked along that it was just as if he were acting out one of Miss Sophia's favorite stories — the one about how she and her young brother Alexander McGillivray had been run out of Georgia because their father was a Tory. They had travelled through the nights like this and hid in the swamps for weeks, till they had finally got back to the Coosa river in Alabama and their plantation home.

Now Gif remembered that on that long journey Miss Sophia had carried her baby son in just such a carrying basket as he had made for Miss Ellie's baby. Gif was proud that his own grandfather had been one of the slaves who had guided Miss Sophia and Alexander back to Alabama. He would tell Miss Ellie that story when they got where it was safe to talk.

Gif took a deep breath. The air was fresh and clean out here on the plains. It smelled like freedom. From the very first day, he'd felt like that fort was an evil place. Yes, Gif was sure glad they had got safely away from Fort Mims!

Historical Notes on "The Whipping"

"The Whipping" is based on a true incident mentioned in all the major Alabama histories. The *Alabama Journal* "Horrible Ft. Mims Massacre Opened Interior of Alabama to Civilization," Montgomery, Jan. 20, 1947, contains the account of Mrs. Durant, 80, "a handsome and distinguished woman," who stated in an interview:

"My grandfather's name was Howard Hall, and he was a tiny, frail baby. His father, Howard Hall, Sr., and my mother had moved into the stockade in 1813 before its completion . . . . One of the Negro boys who warned of the Red Sticks' attack was his slave, and he refused to allow the officers to whip his slave as they did the other one. The slaves had been herding cattle outside the stockade and excitedly reported that Indians in war paint were lurking in the ravine. After being ridiculed by the men in charge, Mr. Hall told his wife to secretly prepare several days' food provisions and make ready to flee. Carrying these and the ailing baby, they slipped out of the fort into darkness. The gates were unguarded and people had gone in and out from the beginning. Traveling only at night and hiding in the swamps at daylight, they traveled 3 days and nights to safety."

On the day after the Halls' escape, 53 men, women and children were killed at FT. Mims.

(On March 3, 1951, the *Mobile Press* reported the death of Mrs. Laura Dolive Durant, aged 98. Born in 1853. She was the widow of Captain N. L. Durant and the granddaughter of Sophia McGillivray Durant. She was survived by 7 children, 31 grandchildren, 41 great-grandchildren, and 2 great-great-grandchildren.)

Sophia McGillivray: A. J. Pickett's *History of Alabama* says of Sophia McGillivray Durant, Alexander's sister:

"During the siege of Savannah she was there with her little boy Lachlan. When the city surrendered to the Americans, she parted from her father, a Tory, in a flood of tears and set out for her native Coosa while he sailed back to Scotland. Some of her father's slaves fled from his Savannah plantations to their former home on the Coosa River to claim the protection of his wife Sehoy." Of Sophia, Pickett said:

"Sophia had an air of authority equal if not superior to Alexander's. She spoke Indian much better, so she often made his speeches to the chief. Her husband, Benjamin Durant of South Carolina, who was of Huguenot descent was a man of astonishing strength. He later became a plantation owner, and Durant's Bend on the Alabama River near Selma was named for him."

David Tate: Dr. M. E. Tarvin's *The Muscogees or Creek Indians,* written by David Tate's grandson, gives details of David's trip to New York with Alexander McGillivray, his schooling and character.

(David Tate's wife, Elouisa, her mother and father, the John Randons, and two of her brothers were killed at Ft. Mims. Peter Randon escaped by leading 16 of his men out of the fort on a scouting mission on the morning of the attack. They were the only survivors. Six years after Elouisa died in the massacre, David Tate married Mrs. Margaret Dyer Powell. Their daughter, Josephine Bonaparte, married J.D. Dreisbach of Baldwin County and they had 14 children. Elouisa and David Tate's daughter, also named Elouisa, married George Brook Tunstall. The second Elouisa's daughter Virginia, famous author of *The Belle of the Fifties*, became the wife of Alabama's well-known Senator, Clement C. Clay.)

—William Weatherford: (Red Eagle) He was the half-brother of David Tate. Pickett's *History of Alabama* states that David was friendly to the United States and opposed to the Creek Indian War. David Tate met his brother William in camp the night before the attack and tried to persuade William to desist. William made a speech to 700 of his warriors and they accused him of treachery when he told them they must spare the women and children. He could not control them, and all in the fort were killed.

—Joe, the runaway slave, was a real person. Pickett says Red Eagle captured 4 Negroes near Claiborne at Zachariah McGrath's plantation. Joe was an intelligent fellow who managed to escape and warn the fort. After several days' fruitless search for Indians, Joe was branded a liar, but he ran away and escaped.

—General Alexander McGillivray: John W. Caughey's *McGillivray of the Creeks* quotes Theodore Roosevelt's opinion that Alexander McGillivray was "the most gifted and remarkable man that ever was born upon the soil of Alabama."

—Jumbo: This is a fictitious name, but Pickett's history states that it was John Randon's Negro who was whipped. He also states that the whipped Negro ran away the next day, so it can be assumed that Jumbo escaped the massacre.

Half-Breed Billy

HIS THIRTEENTH birthday had been the very best day of his whole life, Bud Daly thought as he rode homeward in the late March afternoon. At first he had been a little homesick for the Georgia hills. This new land of Alabama was low and flat, with part of it in swamp and dense pine woods, but he liked these open meadows he was crossing and the giant live oaks hung with Spanish moss that grew along the creek bank. His father said the fields had been cleared for cattle grazing by the Creek Indians who used to own them.

Now he could see his father's red hair and broad shoulders as he and the Negro Lucas plowed the new corn field with the yoked oxen, and he could hear the squeals and laughter of his little tow-headed sisters as they threw scraps to the chickens. A good smell drifted towards him from the log cabin under its sheltering oak and he thought, that'll be Ma's rabbit stew, and kicked his new horse into a trot.

Ma would sure be surprised when he showed her the fine big fish the Indian boy had given him. The nicest thing of all was that he would see his new friend again tomorrow, that is, if Ma would let him go after he finished his chores. Yes, it had been a wonderful day.

First there had been the surprise birthday gift. As Bud had come outside after breakfast to do his woodcutting, his father had come from the shed leading a shaggy little Indian pack horse not much higher than Bud's shoulder.

"A horse! For me?" gasped Bud, afraid to believe his eyes. He had wanted a horse so long. For him it spelled freedom to roam over the new country and to get away from the thousand household jobs his mother could always find for him to do. When his father grinned and nodded, Bud gave a glad whoop and vaulted into the saddle, caressing the rough brown mane as he cantered around the yard, finally pulling up by the log fence that surrounded the garden.

"Thank you, Pa! He's great! I'm going to call him Mutt because his eyes look like that old hound dog we used to have back in Georgia!"

Pa laughed and said that was a good name. "He don't look like much, but Jeb Frazier, the man I traded with, said he would travel twenty-five miles in a day and was used to living off of native grass and young cane. Mebbe we can get you a bigger hoss when you get your growth!"

Bud's face clouded momentarily. He hated it that he was small like his mother. Pa was over six feet tall and was always joking with him that Bud was the runt of the litter. Then Bud realized that on his new horse he was as tall as anybody, and he hurried through his work, eager to be away.

Of course, Pa had been saying all along that if they ever got to Little River, he'd swap the off-ox and get him a horse, but Bud had long ago learned to take most of Pa's promises with a grain of salt. Pa meant well, but things always seemed to go wrong for him.

Bud had driven the three teams of oxen almost all the way to Alabama along the Three-Notch Road while his mother tended to his sick baby brother and the two little sisters back in the wagon. His Pa had ridden the mare Queenie alongside, except that naturally Pa had taken over the driving when they had to ford creeks or got stuck in muddy sloughs. In his secret heart, though, Bud knew that he could handle the big animals better than his father.

Big Jim Daly was noted for his Irish temper, and when he cracked the long whip he was likely to let fly some fancy cuss words at old Tombo, who was about as mean and stubborn as an ox could be. Ma would cover up her ears and plead, "How do you expect me to raise up fine Christian children, Jim Daly, if you can't keep a clean tongue in your head in front of 'em?"

"Sorry, Vinnie, I keep forgettin'," Pa would laugh, "but I 'spect Bud's bound to hear worse where we're goin'. There ain't much parlor language on the frontier."

Bud felt sorry for his Ma. Small and quiet as she was, she was fighting hard to bring them up to be civilized, and it seemed like everything worked against it. The few log houses or taverns where they had taken shelter had been so filthy and the food so coarse and greasy that they had chosen to camp out along the trail unless they were weather-bound.

Bud's Uncle Pete, Pa's younger brother, had written them glowing accounts of the rich parcel of land he had settled on down in the Creek Nation. But then Pete had been killed fighting the Red Sticks at the Battle of Autossee before he'd even had the chance to put in a crop. When Justice Henderson had sent word from Little River that Pete had willed his new cabin to his older brother, right away Pa had got an itching foot and had started talking about getting rid of their worn out hill farm in north Georgia and starting out fresh in the new land.

Ma had tried to hold him back. "I don't like it, Jim," she'd begged. "I'm scared of the savages and the wild varmints in the woods, and there won't be any churches or schools for the young 'uns."

But Pa had just laughed his big booming laugh and set out to talk her around as he always did. "Well, we'll just have to help to build a church and a school if need be, Vinnie. Our luck's been bad enough here these last few years. Maybe down on those rich lands our kids can have a chance to amount to something."

The town of Little River didn't look like much when they finally got there —just a straggle of log houses around the square. The only brick building was Justice Henderson's store. They liked the slender, white-haired old man on sight. He greeted them warmly with a twinkle in his shrewd blue eyes, and gave the children rock candy. Then he invited them into his living quarters to clean up and refresh themselves.

"Most of the news in these parts gets to me sooner or later," he chuckled. "Being as I'm a Justice of the Peace, I do the marrying and settle most of the arguments, and besides that I'm the postmaster and the undertaker." Then he grew serious. "I was sorry to hear of Pete Daly's death. He was a fine young man. But there's hardly a family in these parts that hasn't lost someone at Fort Mims or in one of the other battles. There's still lots of hard talk and bitterness. But the Indians had the worst of it. Last winter lots of them was close to starving, and them that's left around here are plenty peaceable enough now. Most of 'em just want to be left alone to farm their land and build back their houses."

Then Justice Henderson had given them Pete's guns and saddle bags that he'd kept for them in his big storehouse, and Pa had given Bud a small bone-handled knife to wear on his belt. When they had finally reached Pete's small log cabin two miles beyond the town, they had been surprised to see smoke rising from the clay and stick chimney, and even more surprised when three Negroes came shyly around the house, a young couple and an old man.

"Good evenin', Massa," said the grizzled old man. "I'm Uncle Ben and dis heah's my daughter Phemie an' her man Lucas. Mistah Pete, he bought us jes befo' he got hisself kilt, so we jes stayed on heah and put us in a garden. I reckon we b'longs to you folks now."

Ma's people had been Quakers who didn't hold with owning

slaves, but she soon had to admit that Phemie had a way with the little ones. Lucas was just as good with the oxen, and Uncle Ben could tell wonderful stories by the hour. It wasn't long before the Dalys wondered how they had ever gotten along without their Negro helpers.

The biggest disappointment was the log cabin, which was only an empty shell, as Pete hadn't had a chance to finish it. When Ma saw the dirt floor, she put her hands on her hips and got a stubborn look. "Well, Jim Daly, I'm sure you don't expect your family to live in this till it's finished!"

Bud could tell from Pa's sheepish look that he did expect it, but Ma wouldn't be moved. "You and Bud can sleep here if you like," she snapped, "but me and the little 'uns stays in the wagon. What's more, not one speck of my gear is going into that cabin nor am I going to cook a single meal in that fireplace till you've put down a proper floor, and put me up some shelves and a work table. It wouldn't hurt neither if you was to make us a little furniture."

Pa scratched his head, but he knew better than to argue when Ma was in that mood. So the next morning they had all gone to work. Bud had driven the oxen while the men cut trees and snaked them out of the swamp. Then they split the logs down the middle and Bud's father had trimmed them with his foot adz to make a puncheon floor. With the leftover short pieces they made a table and benches and box beds. Finally they had partitioned off two small, windowless rooms, one for Bud and his brother and one for his two little sisters.

Ma had kept them all so busy that this was the very first day that Bud had been able to get more than shouting distance from the cabin. Now he was eager to follow the small creek that bordered his father's land to see whether there were any likely fishing holes.

There was plenty of small game, and he was so intent on following a beaver track that before he realized it, he had ridden past the lightning-blasted tree that marked the boundary of the Daly's land. He started to turn back, but just then he spotted a beaver dam further down the creek which made a pool just right for fishing. He had slid from Mutt's back and gone forward on foot to gaze into the deep, clear water when he saw the boy crouching behind a big boulder. He was about his own size and, like Bud, had light brown hair and gray eyes.

Before Bud could speak, the boy quickly put a hand to his lips for silence and motioned toward the line in his other hand that dangled into the water behind the rock. When Bud had tethered Mutt to a bush and crept forward as quietly as he could, he saw that the line led to a fish trap cleverly fashioned from reeds. Then with a lightning fast movement the boy jerked the cord that shut the door of the trap and pulled it out of the water to show the fine big trout inside.

"Gosh, he sure is a beauty!" exclaimed Bud. "I'm glad I didn't scare him off. I'm Bud Daly. We've moved into my Uncle Pete's cabin up the creek a ways."

"Thank you for being so quiet," smiled the boy. "I've been after this fellow for a long time. Can't catch these big ones on my trot lines, so my father showed me how to rig up this trap."

Bud ran his fingers across the intricate knots of the fish trap, trying to figure out how it was made. "I wish I could make one of these, but it looks plenty complicated."

"If you'd like me to I can show you how, and maybe you'd like to fish with me tomorrow. I'm William Weatherford, by the way, and my father is Red Eagle. We live over yonder at Brickyard Plantation, about a mile downstream."

"I guess everybody's heard of Red Eagle," said Bud admiringly. "I'd love to see him. They say General Jackson called him the bravest man he'd ever seen! But you sure don't look Indian!"

"I'm sort of a mixture," laughed William. "My father is three-quarters English and Scotch, and my mother's father, Grandpa Moniac, was half Dutch. They say I look like him, but I'm prouder of my Creek blood than any!"

Bud was remembering what the old storekeeper had said about some of the Indians starving. This boy certainly looked healthy and well-dressed, he thought. He said tentatively, "Justice Henderson told us some of the Indians had it rough last winter."

William's face clouded. "If so many of our women and children hadn't been starving, my father would never have given himself up to old Jackson Chula Haijo — that's Old Man Jackson in our Creek language. You know Old Jackson said he wouldn't sign a peace treaty until they brought him Red Eagle bound and gagged. My father could have escaped to Florida like some of the others. But he came in on his own!"

"He was sure a brave man to ride in by himself like that," said Bud. "He might have been killed easy, the way most folks around here seem to feel about Fort Mims."

William hung his head sadly. "I know. They call him the Butcher of Fort Mims — but it's not true, you know!" He raised his chin proudly. "His men went against his orders. He was almost killed himself when he tried to stop the slaughter. But seems like people have got to have somebody to blame — an' then there's some bad men around here that would sure like to push the Creeks off of their lands, so they try to keep things stirred up on purpose . . . . They even talk against me!"

William gave Bud a sideways glance that seemed to ask a question. "They call me Half Breed Billy's son. Maybe your Ma won't want you to have anything to do with me."

"Aw, my Ma's not like that," Bud said quickly, though in his heart he recalled Ma's fear of "savages" and decided he would not say too much about his new friendship just at first. "I'd like to come back here and fish with you tomorrow," he said now, "an' I spec' Ma would be real pleased if you could show me how to catch a big fellow like that one!"

William had then insisted that Bud take the fish home to his mother for their evening meal. They had parted on the promise that next day William would be waiting for Bud near the beaver dam.

After that first meeting, Bud met William as often as he could spare the time from his chores. He soon realized that Red Eagle's land holdings were much larger and richer than his own father's. There were forty slaves at Brickyard Plantation, so William was freer than Bud to spend time in the woods and fields.

He taught Bud fascinating things about plants and animals and how to build all sorts of traps and snares. He also taught him how to skin game and prepare the skins so they would not spoil. Later they could be used at the store to swap for trade goods. Bud's mother did not fuss so much now about his absences because he nearly always brought home meat or fish for the table.

Bud would never forget the day he met Red Eagle. He was waiting for William as usual near the fishing hole when he got a strange feeling that someone was watching him. Turning his head slowly, he saw a tall, stern-faced man dressed in fringed buckskins. Even his moccasin-toed boots were made of dressed skins, and a beaded headband with a red feather in it circled his long black hair. He was mounted on the finest gray horse that Bud had ever seen. William had often talked about his father's famous horse, Arrow. There just could not be two horses like that one. Bud stood open-mouthed in silent admiration. "He's beautiful!" he said softly. Then he asked shyly, "Are you Red Eagle, sir?"

"So my people call me," answered the man with a smile that made his lean face pleasant and not stern at all. "Some of the whites call me other names," he added wryly. "William asked me to tell you if I rode this way that he has gone to Pensacola with his Uncle David for a few days."

Bud was so excited by this meeting with the renowned fighter that he hardly knew what he answered. But he could not refrain from the question that was uppermost in his mind. "Please tell me, sir," he asked, "did Arrow really jump off a fifty foot bluff into the Alabama River when you escaped from Ikan Achaka — the Holy Ground?"

The big man laughed, but Bud could tell that he was pleased. "That story gets bigger every time it's told. This fellow made a fine jump, and saved my life with his speed," he patted Arrow's graceful neck, "but the bluff was not more than fifteen feet at that point. I am glad to hear you use the Indian name for the battle."

"William has been teaching me lots of Muscogee words," said Bud proudly. He felt more at ease now with his friend's father and found himself talking eagerly about his new accomplishments.

"William lets me use his bow and arrows, but I'm not as good with them yet as he is, though I can hold my own pretty well with my rifle. He's going to help me make my own bow when we get the chance. And before cold weather comes, he's promised to show me how to make moccasin boots like those you're wearing."

Red Eagle smiled. "You must visit us some day and I will show you my weapons and the ceremonial garments made by our Creek women. I am glad my son has found a companion of his own age. We would like to be good neighbors." Then Red Eagle turned Arrow homeward and raised his hand in farewell. His body looked as if it were molded into the horse, Bud thought as be watched him ride away.

Jim Daly had started out fine on the new farm. He had worked beside the Negroes getting the crops in, improving the outbuildings, and building a springhouse.

Then he had begun to drift back into the old ways that had brought on what he always called his hard luck. He had swapped off another one of the oxen for a stallion to breed to Queenie and had once remarked that he might some day build a racing stable.

"There's talk in town of having a race next year," he had told them one evening as they sat around the table. "They say old Half Breed Billy's father was a rich Englishman who used to have some of the finest horses ever seen in the South. People came from all over everywhere to race against his horses." He nodded wisely. "Believe me, I'd sure like to have the get of the gray horse that Injun rides!"

Bud got a sick feeling inside when he heard his father say "Half Breed Billy" in that scornful tone of voice. Then he thought with relief that there wasn't a chance in a million that Red Eagle would ever breed Arrow to a mare like Queenie. He began to wonder uncomfortably if that was being disloyal to his father.

Bud had not told his parents about meeting Red Eagle. It was something he liked to think back over and enjoy all by himself. Far down inside him there was a fear that he did not like to admit even to himself, a fear that his own father might turn out to be one of the men William had spoken of who wanted to push the Creek Indians out of their homes.

Except for Justice Henderson's store, the blacksmith's shop was the most popular gathering place in town. But no women ever went there, and the men who habitually swapped stories around Zeke's glowing forge were usually of the rougher sort. The chief attraction was a shed behind the shop where Zeke's rheumatic old uncle presided over a barrel of cheap raw whiskey.

Bud did not like the crude jokes and loud talk of these men. It worried him that lately his father had taken to spending time there and coming home late to supper with the smell of spirits on his breath.

But Mutt had cast a shoe, and Zeke was a good blacksmith. As Bud watched the sparks fly from the anvil, he could hear the rise and fall of the men's angry voices back in the shed. Suddenly he recognized the sharply raised tones of Jeb Frazier, the horse trader, a dirty, yellow-faced man whom he specially disliked.

Jeb had a small horse ranch up the river, and William had told Bud that most of Jeb's horses had been stolen from the Indians. Nobody had proved anything against him, however, mainly because they were afraid of the giant strength of his helper, a mean, slow-witted bully named Lum Carter. Lum had the habit of beating up all challengers at the local wrestling contests.

As Jeb's whining voice rose louder, Bud could make out some of the words. "'Tain't right fer that half-breed that led the slaughter of our people to be squattin' on that fine big plantayshun whilst our folks goes hongry," he was saying. "He ought by rights to be run off to Floridy like we run off old McQueen and them others!"

Other voices were chiming in now and Bud stopped listening, but all the way home he kept thinking over what he had heard and wondering if his father felt as Jeb Frazier did. Bud knew that above everything his father admired fighting skill and fine horsemanship. If only Pa had a chance to really know Red Eagle, Bud thought, he was bound to admire him. Jim Daly was a pretty good fighting man himself and a good horseman, too, and most of the time he tried to be fair. But if he got likkered up like he'd been sometimes lately, well, it just didn't bear thinking about.

Bud shivered, then threw back has thin shoulders and kicked Mutt into a canter. The setting sun was casting long shadows in front of him now, and Bud, who was not usually fanciful, felt as if there was a dark shadow on this new land that he was already beginning to love.

A few days later it all happened just as Bud had feared. His father was after dark getting home, and this time someone was riding with him. Bud slipped out to the shed and stayed back of the hay bin until he could make out who the other rider was. He couldn't see the man's face, but he would know those whining tones anywhere. Pa was so unsteady he had to be helped from his horse, and Jeb Frazier was saying, "You be ready now when you hear me sound like a hoot-owl three times. We'll hold off till about midnight — give the moon time to set." He chuckled. "That ole half-breed won't know whut hit him!"

Bud felt himself growing tense with rage. For a moment he felt ashamed of eavesdropping, but right now he felt older than his father. Pa was a good man. It wasn't right for these men to rake him into their dirty business. Then he forgot everything else except his fear for Red Eagle.

Somehow, I've got to warn him, he thought. But if I slip off, my folks will miss me, and besides I don't think I can find my way to Brickyard Plantation in the dark. I wish I'd gone over there when Red Eagle asked me, but I was waiting on William to come home. There just must be some way to let him know.

Suddenly the answer came to him. The Negroes. They went to their own cabin at sundown, and nobody checked on them after that. Bud knew they went over to Brickyard to listen to the Negro preacher on Sundays, and he knew Lucas had kinfolks among Red Eagle's slaves.

Bud could hear his Ma's complaining voice in the lamp-lit kitchen as she warmed up food for his Pa. They wouldn't miss him right away. He hurried to the small cabin behind the garden fence and called softly to Lucas. Beckoning the tall black man into the yard, Bud quickly explained his errand. "Please help me, Lucas. You can ride on Mutt — I've just had him shoed. These men won't bring Pa nothin' but trouble! Red Eagle told me himself he wants to be good neighbors to us. . . . You've just got to go, Lucas. You can go through the pastures and they won't miss you." Bud had an awful feeling that he was very close to tears.

Lucas patted his shoulder. "Don't fash yose'f, boy. I know de way, an' I'll git 'em de word in plenty time. His people all say Red

Eagle's a good mastah, none bettah, an' dis bizness ain' right." He nodded solemnly. "Nawsuh, hit sho ain't!" He patted Bud's shoulder again. "Gwan home now, an' ack like you don' know nuthin'. I'll just tell Phemie, an' won' nobody heah me leave." He brushed off Bud's thanks and slipped quietly back into his cabin.

Later, as he lay in his bed, Bud listened as hard as he could, what with his Pa's snoring and his little sisters chattering, but he heard nothing but the ordinary night noises of the katydids and bullfrogs. He must have dozed off to sleep then because the next thing he was aware of was a hoot-owl calling. Then there was a muffled curse as his father stumbled over a bench beside the front door. For a long time Bud lay awake worrying and trying to follow the night riders in his thoughts. Then he fell asleep again.

It was not until after breakfast that he was able to slip out behind the shed and talk to Lucas. Pa's eyes were all puffed up this morning, and he was real slow getting started. Lucas looked proud and happy, and he was full of admiration for Red Eagle.

"Fust he thanked me fuh de warnin' — an' I didn' see no use tuh tell him yo' Pa wuz mixed up in it a tall!"

"Thank you, Lucas," said Bud softly. "I'm glad you thought of that."

"Den he jes took cha'ge lak he wuz a big genril," Lucas went on. "He wuz postin' his men all aroun', hidin' de stock an' all. Fust off, though, he sent fuh his brudder Jack whut fought on de settlers' side at Fo't Mims. Can't nobody say nothin' agin Marse Jack, so Red Eagle aimed fuh him to take ovah Brickyard while he rode off on Arrow to Fo't Claiborne. He say de captin dere is his fren', an' he'll pertec' him till dese men come to dey senses!" Lucas nodded confidently. "Twon't be long befo' he be back home ergin. Am' nobody gonna git de bes' uv dat man!"

Things around Little River were quiet for a long time after that, and at times Bud thought maybe it was too quiet. The feelings of the troublemakers hadn't changed any, he knew, and he kept wondering what sort of plot they might hatch up next time. Then came the big day of the auction sale when the whole thing broke wide open in front of everybody.

The auction was planned by Justice Henderson to sell off the personal belongings of his deceased elderly cousin, Duncan Henderson, who had lived alone on a small plantation a few miles from town. It was rumored that this old fellow, who was considered to be something of a hermit, had made a hobby of collecting fine weapons. This drew the settlers like a magnet.

On the day of the big sale the dusty little square was a noisy tangle of horses and wagons, pack ponies, women in sunbonnets with broods of big-eyed children, and lean backwoodsmen in buckskins or clean, homespun work clothes.

Justice Henderson had put up long tables full of lamps, china and other household items in the vacant lot next to his store. The storekeeper himself was staying close to the table of weapons that was drawing the biggest crowd.

Bud and William were with a group of younger boys who had started a series of contests in the field back of the auction tables. Bud didn't figure they would have much chance to win the foot races or at wrestling or tossing the log, since William was even smaller than he was.

"Let's enter the archery contest," Bud suggested to his friend. "You're as good as anybody here or better. I'll try it if you will."

Bud was pleased when William agreed. He knew that some of the women did not like their sons to play with William because of their bitterness toward the man they called Half Breed Billy. He was eager now for his friend to show off his skill in archery. "C'mon then," he urged, "and I hope you heat the socks off of them!"

Bud made a fair showing, thanks to William's coaching and his own long hours of practice with his new bow, but his best shot was two inches from the center. Each contestant was to have three shots.

When William made his first bull's-eye, there was a murmur of surprise, for the Indian boy was so quiet and so much alone that he was not often noticed or thought of. At the second and third bull's-eye, Bud could hardly contain himself. He pummeled his friend on the back. "Atta boy, William. That's great!" he shouted, and William's face glowed with pride. Bud happened to look up just then, and beyond William's shoulder he caught the watching eyes of a tall figure on the outskirts of the crowd.

"Your father saw you win!" he murmured happily to William. Then Bud raised his clasped hands towards Red Eagle in a gesture of congratulation, and the Indian leader smiled and started towards them.

Suddenly a woman screamed, and at the same time a hubbub of shouting broke out. Heads swiveled towards the table of weapons where Justice Henderson stood in shocked silence. It took an instant for Bud to grasp what was happening. Then the crowd parted for a moment as frightened people began drawing back, and as Bud raced forward he caught a glimpse of an old man lying on the ground in a pool of blood with a long-handled knife sticking out of the back of his neck. Bud began piecing the story together from what people were saying.

"It's old man Bradberry," That was a woman's tearful voice. "That Jeb Frazier broke a pitcher over his head when they was arguin', an' then that Lum Carter knifed him in the back! Why, that ole man wouldn't hurt a fly!"

The man with her was cursing, "The dirty, rotten bullies! Why the hell can't we get some law in this town!" But nobody was going near the old man's body. Everybody was shrinking further back until soon there was a big cleared space around the murderers. Now Bud could see the two men with their guns turned toward the crowd.

One was Jeb Frazier and the other was a big, brutish fellow Bud had never seen before.

"It's Lum Carter," panted William, who had caught up with him. "I told you they were all scared of him! I bet my father could beat him up, though. These men are all yellow!"

Then, as if William's words had conjured him up, there was Red Eagle standing beside Justice Henderson with his dark eyes scornful. He folded his arms and said in clear, ringing tones, "These, I suppose, are white men's laws. You stand and see a man, an old man, killed and not one of you will avenge his blood. If he had a single drop of Indian blood mixed with that which runs upon the ground there, I would instantly kill these murderers at the risk of my life."

Justice Henderson put his hand pleadingly on Red Eagle's arm. "Help us, Billy. You're the only one who can. I am the law here, but I am not able . . . I beg you to be my deputy."

Red Eagle stared into the Justice's eyes. Then he gazed slowly over the crowd, which had grown suddenly quiet — at the women and children cowering in the wagons and doorways, at his son and Bud Daly looking up at him in eager expectancy, and finally at the two scowling men with their drawn guns. Calmly he shifted his hickory cane to his left hand and drew his pearl-handled dagger from his belt as he moved forward with deliberate steps.

Bud felt his stomach muscles contract in fear, but at the same time his chest felt full of pride. With each slow step the tall Indian took forward, Bud listened in horror for the shot that did not come. He was not even aware that his fingers were digging into William's arm. Red Eagle had almost reached the men when Jeb Frazier screamed in a high-pitched voice that sounded frightened, "Stop! I'll kill you if you take another step!"

Red Eagle stared at him, then calmly stepped forward and commanded in a quiet voice, "Give me your gun."

As if hypnotized, Jeb Frazier meekly handed over his gun. Then Red Eagle clutched Jeb's throat with a strong grip and called for a rope. Quick as a flash, Bud darted into the store, but by the time he got back with rope, the horsetrader was already being trussed up by eager helpers.

Lum Carter had backed off a little way, but he was still cursing and shouting, "You won't tie me up, damn you. I'll kill the first man comes near me."

Red Eagle looked at him in disgust and again started that slow, deliberate walk forward. He had not taken more than three steps when the bully yelled, "I didn't mean you, Billy Weatherford!"

But Red Eagle kept right on walking until he could take the gun out of Lum's shaking hand. This time he used Bud's rope to tie his victim up.

The men were all crowding around now, shaking hands with Red Eagle and all talking at once: "Man, I never in my life seen nuthin' like that!" one man was saying, and "Cool as a cucumber he was — it jes' beat ever'thing!" came from another. Finally they began to drift away, and Red Eagle went into the store with Justice Henderson. Bud and William followed at their heels. Bud heard the Justice ask, "Weren't you afraid, Billy?"

"Noisy, threatening men like that are not the kind of men to be feared," answered Red Eagle. "They wilt when you face them down. They won't fight unless they can come at you in the dark." He looked down at Bud and winked.

He's remembering the night riders, thought Bud, and he suddenly recalled with a flood of shame that his own father had been one of them. Then he became aware that his father was in the store and had heard Red Eagle's words. Now Pa was coming forward, and his voice was gruff with feeling as he shook hands with the tall Indian.

"That was a fine thing you did today." He smiled at the two

boys. "I believe our sons are friends. I am Jim Daly and I am proud to be your neighbor."

That night Bud's father did not visit the blacksmith's shed. He rode home beside Bud, and for a long time they rode in silence. Finally Jim Daly said slowly as if he had given it deep thought, "You know, son, I think that Injun's a really good man. He's got real guts."

"Yes, sir," answered Bud, and thought what a day this had been. He would never forget the way Red Eagle had looked walking toward those guns.

"Say, Pa," he said softly, "Red Eagle invited me over to Brickyard Plantation. He said he'd show me his weapons and his ceremonial costumes."

"That's fine, son, just fine," said Jim Daly. The setting sun cast their long shadows in front of them as they came in sight of the cabin, and Bud gave a contented sigh as he smelled his ma's cooking. Funny, the way things worked out, he thought.

Historical Notes on "Half-Breed Billy"

William Weatherford: See Historical Notes at end of "The Creek Captives" for William's background and early life and characteristics. (From B.J. Riley's *Makers and Romance of Alabama History*," of Alabama History) pp. 530-535:

"After the Battle of Horseshoe Bend, in which he did not participate. William Weatherford returned to Little River where his brother Jack and his half-brother David Tate divided their lands with him and seated him on a plantation (Brickyard) near them. The natives were hostile and plotted to kill him, and he was advised to shelter at Fort Claiborne, upriver, which he did for a few weeks. Later he quietly returned."

pp. 596-597: "Billy Weatherford in 1820 attended an auction sale of deceased Duncan Henderson's effects in the lower part of Monroe County which drew a large number of people of all ages. Two bullies (A. J. Pickett in his *History of Alabama* calls them F____r and C____r) attacked old man Bradberry. . . . One bully broke a pitcher over the old man's head and the other stabbed him in the back of the neck so that he fell dead. Billy saw this. When the two murderers stood in the public square brandishing revolvers and daring the crowd, a justice of the peace (Pickett says Justice Henderson) called on the crowd to arrest them but none dared, for they had long been a terror."

Riley's account says Billy "drew a pearl handled dagger and shifted his hickory stick to his left hand," while Pickett does not mention the stick and says Billy "drew a long silver-handled butcher knife." Both accounts agree that Billy walked slowly toward the murderers and demanded their guns, which they meekly handed over, and then tied them up. Riley concludes: "This brave deed made Billy a hero, and during the remaining twelve years of his life in Little River he turned the people's bitterness into love."

(from George C. Eggleston's William Weatherford)

"William's character was changed by the war. He lived surrounded by his family, industrious, sober, and economical, kind to his slaves, honorable, fastidious. His word was sacred to him. He had remarkable intellectual powers, vivid imagination, and fluent language. He loved to tell stories and drew many listeners.

... When he died in 1826, as a result of a tiring bear hunt in the swamps in which he overtaxed his strength, he left a large family of children who later intermarried with whites and left numerous descendants."

Today there is a large and beautiful state park at Little River. William Weatherford's tomb and monument may be seen in the small cemetery at Old Brickyard Plantation near little River where he once lived. A many-bladed knife belonging to "Red Eagle" was presented to the Alabama Archives and History Department by Weatherford's descendants.

The Stagecoach Ride

EVER SINCE my fourteenth birthday in the summer of 1835 things had been going from bad to worse. But it was that stagecoach ride that changed my whole life. I'd better go back, though, and tell you how it all happened.

We had come into Alabama by ox-train from Georgia two years before — Ma and Pa, my two little sisters and me. It seemed like everybody was rushing in to get some of the new land opened up after the Creek Indian treaty of '32. For a while we got along fine. The land was rich, and we had good neighbors that helped us raise a snug log cabin over near Crocketsville. Ma taught lessons to me and the girls. M'lissa was ten and smart in books, but Minnie was only eight and spent more time on her pet kittens than lessons.

Me, I never cared much for books. I spent most of my time looking after the animals on the place. We had swapped our oxen for a cow, hog and chickens and a couple of Injun ponies. Pa always got along fine with the Injuns. Some of old Tuskoona Fixakoo's tribe was camped over in the woods nearby. Pa traded fair with 'em, and we even had an old squaw named Polly to help Ma around the place.

Our bad luck started when Ma died havin' a baby, and the baby died, too, though old Polly did her best. After that, Pa took to gettin' filled up with firewater most evenin's, and I didn't have the heart to blame him. M'lissa wasn't too bad a cook, an' I took over extra chores around the house like soap makin', grindin' corn on the hand grinder, and buildin' fires. I'd a heap rather been over visitin' with the Injuns, huntin' or trappin', or just explorin' the countryside.

It wasn't more than six months after Ma died when Pa got killed whilst fellin' a tree. He had a gimpy leg from an old bullet wound he'd got back in his soldierin' days and couldn't get out from under fast enough. The neighbors all come 'round bringin' food and consultin' 'bout what was to become of us. The upshot was that they sent word back to Pa's relations in Harris County, Georgia, where we come from. It wasn't long before old Hiram Lackey, Pa's first cousin who was a storekeeper back there, came down to take charge of us.

He drove up one day in a hired buggy, an' he was even fatter than I remembered. I'd only seen him once before when we'd stopped by his store to stock up for the trip to Alabama. He was a monstrous fat man with a shiny beaver hat on his bald head and a flowered vest with a big gold watch and chain across it. He made a big fuss over the girls, huggin' 'em and tellin' 'em how Cousin Susie'd always wanted a little girl to make dresses for, and how he'd give 'em the pick of ribbons and laces out of his store.

I didn't think Cousin Susie'd care much for havin' a boy aroun' the house, though. She was a tall, skinny woman with a long neck and a primped-up mouth, and all she'd ever said to me when we went over there was, "Wipe the mud off yo' feet befo' you come in," and "Wash yo' hands befo' you touch my good things!"

After the girls went up to bed in the loft, Cousin Hiram sat down in Pa's big chair by the fire and says, "Now, son, let's talk a bit about your future and about this place here."

I eased down onto a stool across from him. I was kinda resentful of him sittin' there in Pa's chair and I was worryin' about what was comin' next. Pa and me had talked a lot about what a fine big plantation we'd build that would be mine to carry on after he'd gone. "Some day this land will be full of new towns with schools and churches," he'd tell me, "and we'll be the ones who started it all."

Now here was Cousin Hiram sayin' he already had a buyer in mind who would take the place over sight unseen just on his say so. I jumped up mighty quick at that. "I couldn't go along with that. What kinda man is he with stock? Our cow's kinda used to me an' she won't let just anybody milk her. Anyway, I half promised her to Miz Studsill, who's been mighty good to me an' the girls . . ."

"Just a minute, son," says Cousin Hiram, smoothin' his jaw. "Don't be so quick on the trigger. I didn't like to bring this up so soon, but I've been appointed your legal guardian. After all, I do have a business to get back to, a very flourishing business, I might add, what with all these new settlers pouring in. I had thought I might train you to help in the store. I'm not as slender as I used to be, and it would be a help to have a boy to fetch and carry."

He chuckled at that and his chins jiggled, but I noticed the laugh didn't reach his eyes. I knew then what my future would be, and it gave me a sorta sick feelin', though there wasn't much I could do about it.

I argued some more about the animals, though I'd about lost hope. Finally, though, Cousin Hiram gave in and said he'd take the girls on to Columbus, Georgia, next day, which was only about twenty miles. He'd see his buyer there and tend to some business for his store and leave me here to see to disposin' of the stock. I promised I'd be ready to leave by the end of the week.

Next day the girls packed up their belongings and the things we'd keep, like Ma's fine quilts and her few good pieces of china and silver. It was a sad feeling to see my sisters and Cousin Hiram jogging off down the road in the hired buggy. None of us dreamed then that all hell would break loose the very next day.

The first hint I had of trouble was when old Folly came early to fix breakfast. She'd promised to cook for me when the others left. She was a dirty old woman and smelled pretty strong of Injun, but I was used to her an' didn't pay it no mind. This day she was scared looking and kept jabberin' at me all the while I was eatin' hoecakes and drinkin' coffee.

"You go back Jawja — go now, go quick," she was sayin'. "Yo' maw Inklis — that meant 'good squaw' — an' she been good to me. Go now, 'fore you be kill. Go, go!" Next thing I knew she was runnin' out of the kitchen and slippin' off behind the smokehouse.

It kind of shook me up a mite, but I didn't have nowhere to go till Sat'day mornin' when I'd told Cousin Hiram I'd meet him over to Sheriff Elliott's house, which was the stage stop on the Crawford Road a mile east of our place. Cousin Hiram was to come out by stagecoach on Friday and spend the night at the sheriff's as he had some legal business to tend to. Then we'd go on to Columbus by stagecoach Sat'day mornin'.

Not knowing what else to do, I went on about my chores. I couldn't really believe old Chief Fixakoo had much harm in him unless he was pretty well likkered up, which he sometimes was. I'd heard it said he'd been a tough fighter in the old days, and that he'd sworn to die on his own land. Somehow he'd managed to keep his tribe together and they'd hung on to their land and cattle when lots of the other Injuns was movin' west to the reservation.

When I took the cow over to Miz Studsill's, I found out that old Polly knew what she was talkin' about. The family there was all in an uproar and packin' up to move. Finally I got out of them what had happened. The Injuns had sure enough been on a rampage. They'd burned the bridge on Big Uchee Creek over on the Old Federal Road, had killed Mr. McKizzie and his wife, and also had plundered Mr. Hartwell Green's wagon and killed his mules, though the family got away safe. Joseph Blake had been out with his boys rousin' the neighbors, and ten families was makin' up a caravan to head for Columbus come nightfall.

They wanted me to go with 'em and warned me against goin' home alone. I was mighty tempted to stay there, but I got to worryin' about the ponies. I knew I had to take 'em over to the sheriffs as I'd promised. Likely they wouldn't close the stage stand, else the stage couldn't get through. So I snuck home by the back path, seein' Injuns behind ev'ry bush.

By the time I got there I was too scared to fool aroun' much. I just scraped together some cold food, made a pack of my belongings to strap on one of the ponies, and turned the hogs and chickens loose to fend for themselves. Then I saddled the other pony and lit out for the sheriff's.

The news there was bad, too. The stage out from Columbus had got through all right, but the one from the Old Federal Road was overdue and they feared the Injuns had been layin' for it The sheriff and his two brothers had guns pokin' out the winders. They was right glad to have another hand an' put me to work helpin' to barricade the place.

Along about sundown the stage passengers come up in a rickety old wagon they'd got from somewhere, an' sure enuff, the Injuns had burned the stage and stole the horses. The passengers wasn't hurt none, but they done a heap of complainin'. I looked 'em over and didn't figger they'd be much help, 'cept the driver, who was a mean old cuss. Besides him there was just a real old couple and a pasty-faced woman with two little boys.

I bedded down with the men on the floor of the big room that night, an we took turns keepin' watch but nuthin' happened. Next mornin' the Columbus stage come in on time, and out steps Cousin Hiram. He was red in the face an' his chins shakin', an' right away he starts jawin' at me. "Young man, if you'd come away with me and yore sisters, we'd a been safe at home by now an' out of this damned country!"

It provoked me, him actin' like I was to blame for the Injun uprisin'. Howsomever, it wasn't my place to answer him back, so I just looked at him, an pretty soon he simmered down an' had a couple of drinks That night it come out that what he was really worried about was the money. I heard him tellin' Sheriff Elliott that he'd got paid $1500 for our place, an' that he had it strapped aroun' his big belly in a money belt. Of course, it was rightly my money, too, but the way I had Cousin Hiram sized up, I doubted if I'd ever see much of it.

The main thing that worried me was gettin' outa there with a whole skin, so I was almighty glad to hear the stage horn blowin' next mornin'. It came chargin' in with the four horses all steamed up. Besides them it had three extra hosses tied on behind that was bein' moved out to safety, as they'd had word of another stage bein' waylaid an' burned.

We had a fine big breakfast — fried chicken, battercakes with molasses, an' ham and eggs. I ate plenty, havin' been goin' light on food lately, but I never seen anybody put food away like Cousin Hiram. He had to turn sideways to get in the stage, and when he settled down in his seat, that stage was plumb lopsided.

After we got underway, it wasn't long before Cousin hiram began to snore, an' from the whiskey smell I figgered he'd taken on a good load. I was small for my age, an' ev'ry time we hit a bump, I'd have to hang on to keep from slidin' down against my Cousin Hiram.

Then I happened to look up an' caught the eye of a tall, youngish fellow in a soldier's uniform, sittin' alone in the seat ahead of me. He had wide shoulders and light gray eyes with a laugh in 'em. When he saw I'd noticed him, he gave me a wink and signalled me to move on up and sit with him, which I was glad to do.

"Your father?" he asked me, noddin' towards Cousin Hiram. When he saw my expression at that, he began to laugh, and pretty soon I was laughin', too, the first time I'd laughed in a good long while.

He was easy to talk to, an' before I knowed it I was tellin' him all about Pa and Cousin Hiram an' how he planned to put me to work in his old store. Seemed like I had it all bottled up inside me just waitin' to come out. Then Jim Hardaway, for that was his name, began to tell me about how he was left an orphan, too, when he wasn't much older than me.

He had run off to Texas, where the Mexican government was beggin' for settlers, and had got a job on a ranch breakin' wild hosses. But the Mex government broke its promises to the settlers, and the Texans tried to set up their own government. Then a cruel bandit named Santa Anna took over an' marched in with army, ravagin' the countryside and murderin' ev'ry American in sight.

Finally, just last month, Santa Anna's army had massacred 166 Texans in the Alamo, wounded an' all. Jim got a grim look on his face when he told me this, 'cause lots of these men was his friends. He'd sold hosses to Jim Bowie and had met Colonel Travis and Davy Crockett, all of 'em I'd give anything to see.

"I was on my way to join up with the Texas defenders," he told me, "when I got arrested and thrown in jail. It was a stinkin' dirty adobe an' I near 'bout starved, but I guess it saved my life at that. 'Cause if I hadn'ta been arrested, I'd been killed in the Alamo with the others."

He sighed and looked out the window like he was seein' things that wasn't there. Meanwhile, I was studyin' him an' likin' what I saw, thinkin' to myself that this was the kind of man I wanted to grow up to be, a tough man who knew how to laugh and who would fight for his friends.

We rode along peaceful like for awhile. It was a sunny day in May, not much dust on the road and a smell of flowers comin' in the open windows. I was about to doze off when all of a sudden

Jim grabbed my arm and signalled me to be quiet. He was peerin' out into the tall canes that grew close to the road as we come up to Brush Creek. "Look close to the right of that dead tree yonder, an' don't make a sound."

Then I seen it, a feather that wasn't on no bird, an' when I looked closer I seen a naked arm through the cane. All this happened in seconds, an' before I had half taken it in, Jim was out of his seat and leanin' over me, pressin' a small pistol into my hand. "Are we partners, kid?"

"Of course. Let me come . . ."

"No, listen and do exactly as I say. Can I count on that?" And when I nodded he went on, "Then give me a minute with the driver. When I jump down I'll rap on the coach and that's your signal to cover me. Shoot towards that cane beside the dead tree, then get the passengers down to the ford below the bridge." Then he pressed my shoulder and swung out the door.

It didn't seem no time at all till I heard Jim's signal, an' I let go real careful at where I'd seen the Injun feather. By the time I'd got off two more shots, ev'rybody was yellin' and screamin', and Cousin Hiram was makin' sounds like a man comin' up from drownin'. Then the coach stopped with a jerk an' the passengers was all spillin' out on the side away from the bridge. Cousin Hiram got stuck in the door an' by the time I got him pulled out, the others was scatterin' like a covey of quail.

I heard Cousin Hiram puffing along behind me. Then I stopped hearin' him and when I got to cover I looked back. He was all sprawled out on his back with an arrer through his throat. I given thought to tryin' to drag him a piece and to the money belt. But it woulda took two big men to move him an' the others was long gone. So I took out after 'em, figgerin' I'd best get away from there whilst the Injuns was busy with the hosses.

All this time I'd been hearin' Jim shootin' from the canebrake, easy and careful like he was movin' after each shot. I wished I was there with him, an' I wondered if I'd see him agin. He'd given me a job to do, though, and I'd try to do it.

After we'd splashed across the ford 'bout half a mile downstream, the old couple and the littlest boy began to give out. The stage driver was helpin' the old lady, so I taken up the boy so he wouldn't hold us up none. Time to time I'd run ahead to find a sheltered place fer 'em to rest. We wasn't more than seven or eight miles from Columbus, but it was hours later and near sunset before we straggled into town.

That place was plumb full of refugees from west of the river. When we'd fed and rested, an' I'd found the tavern where Cousin Hiram had lef' Minnie an' M'lissa, folks begun crowdin' 'round to ask questions. I tole 'em all about Jim Hardaway an' how he'd stayed behind an' held off the Injuns so we could get away. When they heard about Cousin Hiram gettin' killed an' about the $1500, they took up a collection for me an' the girls to pay our lodgin' bill, which was a dollar a piece for each night, an' for stage fare to get us on to Cousin Susie's in Harris County.

The girls was wore out with all the excitement and wanted to go on to their new home an' get settled. I jus' couldn't bring myself to leave without hearin' how Jim made out with them Injuns. Finally next morning I decided to send the girls on to Cousin Susie's in the care of a kind lookin' gray-haired lady that was goin' that way. Then I settled down to wait, gettin' more an' more worried as the hours went by.

It wasn't till pitch dark the next day that he finally came in. He'd killed four Injuns, he told us, by sneakin' up on 'em in the cane. He wasn't wounded himself excep' bein' all scratched up by briars an' his clothes was so tore up he was half naked. By the time Jim Hardaway come in, ev'rybody had heard my story an was ready to treat him like a hero.

They took up a collection for him, too, enough to buy him a fine new outfit of clothes and to pay his fare home to Macon. Then they treated us both to a big dinner, an' I was mighty proud when Jim give me the credit fer helpin' him. "If it hadn't been for my young partner coverin' me from the coach, I might not've been able to get into position in time to do much good," he told 'em.

Then they had to hear all about the fightin' down in Texas. Plenty of 'em had friends down there, so it was late when we went up to the room I was sharin' with Jim. I was so glad to have Jim back safe that I wouldn't have thought anything could make me happier. But I was wrong.

When we got upstairs Jim says, kinda laughin', "I take it you're not in any hurry to go to store keepin'?"

"I don't even want to think about it," I told him.

"Then how would you like to come work for me in Macon? You say you're good with animals. I was thinkin' of breedin' hosses on my grandpa's place. He's old and sick an' wants me to take over."

For a minute there I couldn't say a word. Then I let out a whoop that woulda woke the dead.

All of that was a good many years back, but now you see how it come about that a stagecoach ride changed my whole life. And that's how I come to be Jim Hardaway's partner on this here fine horse ranch.

Historical Notes on "The Stagecoach Ride"

Tuskoona Fixakoo's Raid (*Alabama: A Documentary History*, Lucille Griffiths, U. of Ala. Press, 1968, taken from Hist. of Opelika, Rev. F.L. Cherry, 1886)

"On May 9, Uncle Blake Thomas and his servants were plowing when they discovered Tuskoona Fixakoo and his son driving their cattle toward their council house or wigwam, an unusual occurrence. . . .

"The only house on the Crawford Road between Uncle Blake's and Columbus was at Crocketville, a mile east of Crawford, and was Sheriff George W. Elliott's. Blake's brother Joseph was on the Crawford Road and saw people leaving because Indians had burned the bridge on Big Uchee Creek on the Old Federal Road, killed McKizzie and his wife, and plundered Mr. Hartwell Green's wagon and killed his mules. Green and his slaves and family escaped. Joseph returned home by night and roused the neighbors. . . . By 9 p.m. the caravan (of 10 families) started from John Perry's house north of the creek . . . and got to the river at Hardaway's Ferry about daylight May 10, 1836."

The Stagecoach Ambush (*Alabama: A Documentary History*, Lucille Griffiths) and Death of Mr. Lackey:

"On May 12, Tuskoona Fixakoo waylaid and burned 3 stages, each with 4 horses and 3 led horses and stole the treasure of the stage company. . . .

"In the ambush at Brush Creek all the passengers escaped except Mr. Lackey of Harris County, Georgia, who was so corpulent he could not get away. He was the agent for some orphan children and had $1500 on him which was lost when he was killed."

Hardaway: (*Alabama: A Documentary*, Lucille Griffiths)

"Among the passengers was a soldier named Hardaway, returning from Mexico after an imprisonment by Santa Anna over the Texas trouble. Well armed and game, he fought at his leisure, giving the other passengers time to escape and killing several reds. Hardaway hid in the canebrake, which was thick at the time, and killed 4 Indians with his pistol as they crept upon him . . . . He got to Columbus nearly naked three days later, and the people gave him new clothes and a ticket for Macon."

Stagecoaches (*Tuscaloosa, Alabama: Its Early Days*, M.W. Clinton, Tuscaloosa, 1958)

"By 1830 all main towns had post roads and stage lines. The coaches were stoutly built, the roads rough and dusty. The avenge speed was 4 miles an hour and the fare was ten cents a mile. The coaches had 4 to 6 horses, and coach 'stands' were 10 to 16 miles apart. Eating houses were placed at the 'stands'."

Tavern Rates: (*Flush Times in Alabama and Mississippi*, Joseph Glover Baldwin)

"In 1840 at the Indian Queen Hotel in Talladega, a meal was twenty-five cents, lodging for man and horse a dollar per night and board per month nine dollars."

Ride a White Horse

"WE MUST be almost there," gasped Lon as he rested on his oar. "I can smell it already." A wide grin lit his freckled face as the foul odor from his grandfather's tannery drifted down the river.

"Hit's jes eround de nex' bend," answered the small black boy in the back of the rowboat, whom Lon affectionately called Skinny. "Uncle Josh sho be glad ter git dese hides we's bringin'," said Skinny, mopping his face. "He say if de Yankees come through here, dey won't be no kind of animals lef in Alabama, and den whut will de folks do fer shoes?"

"Ma says some of our soldiers are almost barefooted already," answered Lon sadly. "Seems like this old war has gone on forever. It began when I was six an' I'm 'most twelve now. We haven't heard from Bill or Tom in two months. Ma's gettin' pretty worried."

Lon grasped the oar again. "We'd best move along. Maybe Uncle Josh will have some news. There isn't much he doesn't find out about."

The heavy rowboat with its load of fresh hides began to move upstream slowly. It was a warm day in early April, and the Black Warrior river was swollen with the spring rains. Lon had enjoyed the trip down river in the early morning. It had been interesting talking to the old trapper about the animals of the swamps. Now the noon sun was beating down on his aching back and his belly felt empty. He hoped Ma would have some hot cornbread and bacon drippings.

As the rowboat rounded the last bend, Lon could see the sprawling sheds of the tannery and the rows of open vats full of evil-smelling tannic acids. He remembered how he had hated the place when Grandpa had first hired him to work on weekends and after school. Many of the Negro workers had run away to join the Yankees, and with Lon's brothers off fighting with Forrest's cavalry there was almost nobody left here except crippled old men like Uncle Josh and One-armed Moses.

Lon wasn't afraid of hard work. He had been an errand boy for Uncle Will in the fine shoe store uptown ever since he was old enough to make change. The tannery smell took some getting used to, but when Skinny introduced him to the complicated processes the hides had to go through before they turned into soft, pliable shoe leather, Lon became fascinated with the business. Now he knew almost as much as Skinny.

On the way to Uncle Josh's shed, the heart of the tannery, where the leather was stretched and oiled for finishing into fine boots, the two boys passed the series of pits, and Lon was proud that he knew what was happening in each one. He and Skinny unloaded their boat beside the first pit, the greenish, scummy-looking lime bath which would take the hair off the fresh hides.

Each day the hides would be moved forward, first to the suspender pits where One-armed Moses and his helpers would lift them around until they were colored evenly. Then they would go to the floater pits to be laid flat and shifted around with tanners' hooks until they were ready to be pulled out, allowed to dry, and finally dusted with oak acids and stored away ready for bleaching.

Uncle Josh knew everything there was to know about leather. Lon had often heard Grandpa say he couldn't run the business without old Josh. He had been a slave on the Murphy tract, one of old Mr. Jemison's lumber plantations, until his legs were crushed by a falling tree. Then he had been hired out to the Foster tannery and had become such a good bootmaker that he had purchased his freedom long ago. Lon reckoned that must make Skinny free, too, because Uncle Josh had looked after him since his parents had run off to join the Yankees.

As soon as they stood in the open doorway of the finishing shed, Lon knew that something had happened. In the shadows behind the big finishing rollers, he could barely see Uncle Josh's bald pate with its fringe of white hair. Uncle Josh looked scared, and he didn't say a word about the fresh hides they had brought in. Instead he beckoned the boys over to him with a finger to his lips. "Hunch down here beside me real quiet," he whispered. "Both of you promise you won't say nothin' to nobody till we figger whut's bes' ter do!"

"Course we promise, Uncle Josh," said Lon impatiently. "What is it? Are the Yankees coming?"

"They's been a battle at Vance 'bout twenty miles from here. That was three days ago, an' some of them Yankees was kilt by a bunch of Forrest's men. So then the Yanks — Croxton's Raiders, they call 'em — lef de main road an' headed fer de river, aimin' ter cross it an' slip into town by de back door, you might say. But, Skinny," and here he put his arm across Skinny's thin shoulders, "I got some bad news fer you personal, so maybe you boys better slip back here into de storeroom. Come in real quiet now, an' I'll let yo' Pa tell you hisself." Uncle Josh hobbled forward on his crutches and opened the storeroom door.

"Pa's back? You got him hid back here?" whispered Skinny, his eyes looking enormous in his small face. Lon was beginning to see the reason for all the secrecy. Jonah was a runaway slave, and Uncle Josh wanted no trouble with the law. Poor Jonah was a pitiful sight as he crouched in a corner of the storeroom. He had been a big jolly man when he left. Now he was shrunken and starved looking, and his homespun clothes were covered with mud and filth. He put his aims around Skinny as he sobbed, "Yo' Ma's gone, boy. She was drownded crossin' de ribber. I tried my bes' but I couldn' save her. Six of our people drownded an' two of de so'jers. I wish I'd nebber lef' heah, but yo' Ma she would go! She kep' dreamin' 'bout freedom, an' de free land dat dem city men come promisin' us. De only thing dem so'jers evah gib us wuz de leavin's of whut dey stole fum de po' hongry country folks. An' now yo' Ma's gone, an' we still ain't free . . ."

Uncle Josh laid a gentle hand on Jonah's drooping shoulder. "Emmy's free now, son. An' Mistah Will knows you is a good sawmill man. I spec' he let you earn yo' freedom like he did me. He ain' got many good people lef'."

Jonah groaned. "I ain' tole you all of it yet. Dem Yankees is headed fer Mistah Will's home place 'cross de ribber, to take it fer dey headqua'ters. Dey know Cherokee's de riches' plantation fer miles aroun'. Colonel Croxton wuz so mad since Gen'ral Forrest kilt dem men at Vance he'll probly burn up dis whole town! An' another thing! He heard de Senator was headed dis way, an' he's aimin' to capture Marse Robert fust thing he do. I heerd all dis whilst I wuz cookin' dey meals. But de night after Emmy drownded, I snuck out fum camp an' stole one of dey rowboats to search de banks nex' mawnin'. Mistah Will an' Marse Robert wuz allus good to dere people. I don' hold wid all dis burnin' an' killin'!"

"Amen, son," nodded Uncle Josh sadly, "but now we has to be real careful an' plan how to git de news aroun'. You bettah stay hid till I ask Mistah Will kin you go back to de sawmill."

At this point Uncle Josh remembered that Senator Jemison's new boots were ready. He had labored over them for weeks, sponging them with fats and oil to make them supple and smooth. The Senator had joked that he would slip through the whole Yankee line for a pair of uncle Josh's boots, and now it looked like he would have to do just that.

Finally it was decided that Lon and Skinny would deliver the boots to the Senator's new town house and warn him of Croxton's threats. Meanwhile, Uncle Josh would borrow Grandpa's horse and send One-armed Moses over the river bridge to warn Marse Will Jemison at Cherokee to hide his valuables.

A short time later Lon and Skinny, breathless with excitement, rushed toward the Senator's carriage house where old Ocie Taylor lounged against the mounting block mending a frayed whip. On the way they had decided that they would need Ocie's help to save the Senator, who was notably stubborn. As they poured out their story, Ocie scratched his gray head thoughtfully. "Po' Marse Robert! He done jes' got through travelin' all the way fum Virginny an' ain' had but two days' rest. Well, guess dey ain' nuthin' he can do but hide out somewhere. He cain' fight de Yankees all by hisself. Am' none of ouah so'jers in town 'cept a few at de college, an ain' none of dem ovah sixteen . . ."

As the old Negro hurried toward the kitchen door, Lon noticed that the yard of the big new mansion was starting to look neglected. Nobody seemed to be around, and he supposed the gardeners and the younger grooms had all run away like Jonah.

The small cottage where Lon lived with his widowed mother and little sister was not far away, so Lon had watched the great house being built. It was in the style of an Italian villa with a small central tower and lacy balconies. He thought it must be the most beautiful house in the whole state, and when he had seen Miss Cherokee, the Senator's daughter, out riding in the carriage with her fancy parasol and her ruffled dress, he was sure she must be the prettiest girl anywhere. Of course, Ma used to look young and pretty, too, back before Daddy died. But he hadn't seen Ma laugh in a long time now.

Suddenly he felt Skinny nudging him with his elbow, and he saw them coming out the back door. The Senator was arguing with old Ocie, but Lon was relieved to see that he was muffled in an old hooded hunting cloak which hid his uniform.

"I just don't feel right about leaving them, Ocie," he was protesting. "Maybe I could hide in the cellar."

"Marse Robert, you know dey'll look dere fust thing, lookin' fer wine an' whiskey. Dem Yankees say you is like a fox. Wal, when a varmint comes toward a foxes den, de ole he-fox heads off fer de woods ter draw de varmint away fum de she-fox an' de young'uns. You gotta out-fox dem Yankees!" Old Ocie nodded sagely.

This gave Lon an idea, and he said tentatively. "Sir, me an' Skinny went down the river this mornin' to a trapper's cabin in the swamps. Old Ben knows that swamp like the back of his hand. We could take you in the rowboat, an' then we'd come back an' help Ocie guard the house."

"That sounds like a right sensible plan, young fellow. Aren't you Will Foster's grandson? And who's this boy with you? It's of vital importance, you know, that none of this gets talked about . . ."

"Oh, Skinny is Uncle Josh's grandson that helps him in the tannery. Uncle Josh sent us to help you any way we could."

After a short discussion Lon's plan was agreed upon. It was decided that Lon would run home for a quick lunch while Skinny helped Ocie with the carriage. Meanwhile the Senator would explain matters to his wife and daughter. Lon caught a glimpse of their worried faces at a back window as he hurried off toward his home.

He supposed he would have to tell Ma about Jonah and about hiding the Senator. He could trust her, and maybe she could keep watch on the Jemison house in case the Yankees came before he got back.

As he ran, Lon felt his stomach knotting up and he wondered whether it was from fear and if this was the way his brothers felt before they went into battle. He didn't know what he would do if he saw any Yankees, but maybe he would think of something.

Late that afternoon, as he and Skinny hunched tiredly on boxes in the doorway of Uncle Josh's shed, Lon was thinking that this had been the longest day of his life. "This waiting is the worst of it," he said to Uncle Josh, "and not knowing when they're coming."

"We know dey's ovah dere," said Skinny with a shiver, "cuz we seen some bluecoats waterin' dey hosses t'other side de ribber. Dey didn' see us, cuz we hid de boat behin' some willow bushes."

"We've done all we kin, I reckon," said Uncle Josh sadly. "Marse Robert is hid, de warnin' is spread aroun', an' old Captin' Eddins has got about a dozen home guards up on de bridge plannin' to tear up de planks. Hit's a shame it have to be tore up. Skinny, yo' Pa and Marse Robert's other sawmill han's built that bridge outa de bes' heart pine, an' dey done a good job uv buildin'!"

They glanced toward the covered bridge spanning the Black Warrior river above the tannery. In the gathering dusk they could barely make out a few moving figures and a flickering lantern. Suddenly Lon heard his name shouted.

"There's Granpa hitchin' up the buggy," said Lon. "Uncle Josh, can Skinny come home with me to help guard the Senator's house? Ocie can hide us in the barn and we can take turns sleeping like the soldiers do."

"Wal, now, I don' s'pose it ud do no harm, though whut you boys kin do to stop dem so'jers I dunno!" He chuckled.

Lon had to admit to himself as he and Skinny jogged homeward in the buggy that he hadn't figured out yet what they could do against the Yankees. He still got scared when he thought about it. Then he remembered the Senator hiding down in the swamp and he imagined himself having to go back down river and telling Mr. Robert his fine new house was burned. It just didn't bear thinking about.

All through the long night hours when it was his turn to keep watch from the Jemison stable, Lon kept trying to puzzle out a plan. Finally he could no longer keep his eyes open so he poked Skinny awake and tumbled into the bundle of hay they had forked down from the hayloft. "Now you be sure to wake me up if anything happens," he mumbled sleepily, and Skinny crossed his heart and promised faithfully.

It seemed only minutes but was actually two hours later that Skinny was frantically shaking him awake. "Look yonder t'ward de ribber, Lon! Ain' dat sompin' on fire?"

It was true. A red glow spread across the sky to the north of the town. Faintly in the distance came a popping sound that might be gunfire, then a whole series of pops close together. "It's them! They're coming!" yelled Lon.

For a frozen moment the two boys stared at each other. Then Skinny put his arm across his face and his shoulders bowed in a sob. "Whut if it's de tannery burnin'? Now my mama's done drownded an' I'm worried 'bout Uncle Josh. I - I'm scared."

A moment earlier Lon, too, had been petrified with fear, but now the need to comfort his friend brought back a little of his self control. He put his hand on the smaller boy's thin shoulders. "Listen, Skinny, if it'll make you feel better to know Uncle Josh is all right, whyn't you slip down there and see? Then you can come back and tell me what's happened. We oughtn't to both leave, but I can wake up Ocie if they come here before you get back."

Lon had decided that you got more scared when you were waiting for things. He was eager to go down town himself, but right now Skinny needed a job to do to take his mind off his troubles, and he was used to doing whatever Lon wanted him to do.

After Skinny had slipped off into the shadows, Lon settled himself for another long spell of waiting. Seems like that's all I've been doing, he thought, and he began trying to remember what his brother Tom had told them about General Forrest's method of fighting. He could remember some of it: "Hit them befo' they hit you" was one of his sayings, and "Always do the unexpected." Forrest's cavalry had done pretty well with their hit and run tactics, thought Lon. Those Yankees never knew where he'd strike next. But I don't have any troops . . .

The blackness was starting to fade, and Ma's rooster was crowing by the time Skinny got back and flung himself down to catch his breath. "Twan't the tannery," he gasped finally. "Fire wuz de hat fact'ry 'cross de ribber. Some of de Yankees done already come ovah de bridge. Dey jes about kilt Cap'n Eddins an' anothah man. Paw snuck up close in de rowboat an' saw 'em carryin' him off.

"Den jes' as I wuz on de way back here, some uv de college boys wuz marchin' t'wards de bridge tryin' to stop de Yankees, but dey couldn' do nothin'." He sighed. "Dey's such a heap uv dem Yankees. Dey jes' come right on! Wasn't nothin' dem boys could do but run off. When I see de Yankees makin' camp in dat big field jes down de road, I come on back."

He pointed toward town. And now Lon could smell woodsmoke on the freshening wind of early dawn. It looked like it was going to be a fine morning. Lon shuddered. "Le's slip over to my house and get a bite to eat. They won't start anything before full daylight, and we can think better on a full stomach." Lon could hear Ocie rattling pans in his quarters behind the stables. It was going to be an important day, and he still hadn't thought of a plan.

As they sat on the back steps hastily eating the cold hoe cakes Lon had found in his mother's pantry, Skinny suddenly remembered something. "I mos' forgot to tell you 'bout Marse Foster's hoss. Uncle Josh say we bettah hide ole Betsy cuz come mornin' dey won't be no hosses or mules in dis whole town."

They talked over the new problem for some time, but no hiding place they could think of seemed safe. Finally Lon said, "Grandpa can't walk much any more. He couldn't even get to work without old Betsy. He might know some place we could take her. Maybe I better wake him up anyway so he won't think the Yankees have stole her." He tiptoed quietly back into the sleeping cottage, returning shortly with a relieved grin. "He thought of a swell place. You know the old ravine down by the ball field? We went down there one time picking blackberries."

At Skinny's nod he continued, "It's deep enough so she won't even show. Ole Betsy's so tough the stickers won't bother her none, but they'd sure scratch up those Yankees!"

"How 'bout us gettin' all scratched up?" moaned Skinny.

"Tell you what. I'll run get us some old raincoats to cover us up, and we'd better hurry. It's 'most daybreak already."

The ravine was only a short distance away, but they decided to save time by riding Betsy bareback. Soon the old white horse was safely staked out in the gully and the boys were back at their post in the carriage house in time to warn Ocie to hide the Senator's gelding.

By the time Mattie, the Jemisons' fat cook, and Sukey, the housemaid, came from their quarters to start breakfast, rumors of the night's happenings had spread through the town. Mattie looked frightened, and nervous little Sukey was almost hysterical. It took all Ocie's patience to get them calmed down. Later in the morning word came that the Yankees were burning the university, and Lon got a sick feeling in the pit of his stomach. This was it. The burning had begun now, and soon it would be coming this way.

As the endless morning wore on, Lon's admiration for Mrs. Jemison grew. She acted just as though it were any ordinary day, as calm and pleasant as could be. When Ocie told her how the boys had helped the Senator, she came into the yard to thank them. Later Miss Cherokee came out with fresh-baked molasses cookies. Lon thought she looked prettier in her calico morning dress than in the one with all the ruffles. The cookies were a real treat, too. Lon couldn't even remember when he had last had any sugar, and Ma was saving her last bit of molasses to sweeten the coffee.

It was just as they finished the cookies that the Yankees came. Lon had been enjoying them so much that he'd forgotten to keep a lookout, and then suddenly here came a whole troop of bluecoats galloping up like they owned the street. They were banging on the front door now. Lon and Skinny could hear them all the way back at the stable.

"C'mon quick! Let's run hide in the shrubbery out front so we can hear 'em." Lon grabbed Skinny's arm and they scooted around the house and peered fearfully around the edge of the columned porch.

To Lon's surprise the captain was not in the least the brutal, savage-looking man he had expected to see. He was young and pleasant looking, and when Mrs. Jemison came to the door, he looked like he was apologizing, though Lon couldn't hear the words. He could hear plainly, though, when the captain turned and shouted orders to his men to search the house. There was not a thing he and Skinny could do about it — not a thing!

In a little while the captain and Mrs. Jemison were back on the porch, and she was still just as calm as anything, though her face was white and scared-looking. Then it came, just as Lon had known it would all along. The captain was saying, real clear and stern but like he hated to say the words, "I'm sorry, ma'am, but we have orders to burn this house."

Mrs. Jemison was answering something Lon couldn't make out, and then he heard the captain again: "Well, ma'am, we'll allow you fifteen minutes to gather your personal possessions."

Fifteen minutes, Lon thought. What could he do? Then suddenly, as though it had been waiting there in his head all along. Lon had his plan.

It was all falling into place . . . do the unexpected . . . they were scared of Forrest and didn't know where he was. He pulled Skinny quietly away, gasping an explanation as they ran. "We got to get Betsy. Hurry!"

A few minutes later startled residents of Tuscaloosa ran out of doors or poked heads out of windows as an old white horse came galloping down the street, ridden bareback by two small boys who were shouting at the top of their voices, "Forrest is coming! Forrest is coming! The cavalry's right down the road! Hurray for Forrest!"

The young captain's men did not wait for orders. They wanted no more meetings with Forrest. They were mounting their horses before Old Betsy and her burden were out of sight.

Late that night Lon and Skinny sat forlornly beside Uncle Josh on a great mound of finished hides, all that they had managed to save from the burning tannery. It had made a tremendous blaze because of all the oil around the place. High above them over the Warrior River the covered bridge was still blazing. That had been the last act of Croxton's Raiders, setting fire to the bridge as they rode out of town.

Uncle Josh tried to console the boys. "Hit don't mattah 'bout dem old shackledy sheds no way. Dey kin be built back 'thout no trouble. But Marse Robert's fine house now — hit took fo' or five years to build hit, an' you boys done a fine job savin' it. You sho' did!" He began to chuckle, and pretty soon Lon and Skinny were laughing, too.

It had been the longest and scariest day of his life, thought Lon, but he was proud, too. There was one special thing he remembered that made him feel good inside. Just as they were galloping Old Betsy past the Jemison house, his Ma had come running out. She was cheering and laughing and she looked happy and young. He hadn't seen her look like that in a long, long time.

Historical Notes on "Ride A White Horse"

The Tannery (from M.W. Clinton's *Tuscaloosa, Alabama, Its Early Days*)

"Charles M. Foster was a first-class mechanic, and it was a real luxury to wear a pair of his nicely fitting boots. . . . His tannery was established on the bank of the river, and in the 1850s was doing a flourishing business in the tanning of hides and turning out oak tanned leather for all purposes. . . . Foster's tannery was burned by Croxton's Raiders in 1865 and was rebuilt by 1911. In 1814 Foster closed out his business because of old age and ill health."

Clinton also states: "In his factory Foster employed slaves, many of whom were crippled."

Robert Jemison's House (from "Cherokee Place" in *Historic Homes of Alabama*)

"In the late fifties, Senator Robert Jemison sent to Philadelphia for an architect named Lewis, and built, by the work of his own slaves, with materials cut from his own forests, a true to type Italian villa . . . with cupola and Italian blinds. . . . It was built of brick and finished in lumber manufactured at his own saw and planing mill."

The White Horse Incident: (from *Historic Homes*)

p. 93: "Through a boyish trick this home escaped destruction in the War Between the States. It was from old Cherokee Place, seized as headquarters, that Croxton's raiders swept down upon Tuscaloosa. It was upon old Jemison bridge that a handful of boyish cadets from the University of Alabama made their vain and tragic stand . . . when the invaders put to the torch the University and most of the business section of the city.

"It so happened that Robert Jemison, at that time, was at home from the Confederate Senate at Richmond. This became known to the Yankees, and a squad was sent to the house to arrest him. They searched the house without success. A trusted negro servant, Ocie Taylor, had driven him several miles out of town where he had concealed himself in a nearby swamp. . . . The officer in command ordered the Jemison house burned. Mrs. Jemison, then thirty-four years of age, related that the young lieutenant in charge was a gentleman. He generously granted Mrs. Jemison fifteen minutes grace in which to have her valuables moved to safety. It was in that narrow margin of time that two mischievous boys, mounted double upon an old white horse, came galloping up Greensboro Avenue from the direction of Selma, at which place the Confederates were known to be, yelling "Forrest is coming, hurrah for Forrest! . . ." The torches were dropped, and the incendiaries fled over the bridge which they burned behind them.

The Battle at Vance" (from M.W. Clinton's *Tuscaloosa, Ala., Early Days*)

"Near Vance, on March 31, Croxton by accident encountered General Jackson's Brigade of Forrest's cavalry. . . . In the battle several of Croxton's men were killed and thirty captured. . . . Croxton decided to approach Tuscaloosa from a different direction and headed toward the Warrior River. . . . The river was swollen and there was only one ferry boat; Croxton had many extra horses; and there were many Negroes following his army. Consequently the crossing was slow. Several men and horses were lost in the crossing.

"On Monday morning, April 3, Croxton started for Tuscaloosa. . . . In the confusion that attended the crossing of North River, several more were drowned.

"There were twelve home guards stationed at the north end of the bridge that night. On hearing the church bell they immediately began tearing up the floor of the bridge. Among the guards was Captain Ben

Eddins, a retired Confederate officer, who was mortally wounded in the skirmish that followed."

An ironic sequel to the burning of Tuscaloosa in Croxton's Raid is that "a few days after the raid, news of Lee's surrender reached Tuscaloosa. The Confederacy was no more."

Bibliography

Ball, Rev. T.H., *Clarke Co., Ala. and Its Surroundings*, Tuscaloosa, Ala., 1879

Brannon, Peter A., "Echoes of the McGillivrays," *Montgomery Advertiser*, April 23, 1945

____, *Milestones along Alabama's Pathway*, Paragon Press, Montgomery, Ala. 1931

Brown, Virginia P., and Helen Akens, *Alabama Heritage*, Strode Publishers, Huntsville, Ala., 1967

Brewer, Willis, *Alabama, Her History and Resources from 1540 to 1872*, Montgomery, Ala., 1872, aided by George Gaines

Carney, Mary O., *The Yankees Take Over the Easter Shore*, Oct., 1949, Daphne, Ala.

Caughey, John Walton, *McGillivray of the Creeks*, Oklahoma Press, 1938

Claiborne, J.F.H., *Life and Times of Andrew Jackson*, Philadelphia, 1817

____, *Mississippi as a Province, Territory*, and State, Power and Barksdale, Jackson, Miss., 1880

Dreisbach, James D. (descendant of David Tate) biographical sketch in Ala. Archives and Hist. Library

Duffee, Mary Gordon, *Sketches of Alabama*, U. of Ala. Press, 1970

Eggleston, George Gary, *Red Eagle*, Dodd, Mead and Co., N.Y., 1878

Garrett, William, *Public Men of Alabama*, Atlanta, 1872

Gatschet, Albert S., *Towns and Villages of the Creek Confederacy*, Brown Printing Go., Montgomery, AL, 1901

Halbert, N.S., and T.H. Ball, *The Creek War*, Montgomery, 1893

Hemperly, Marion R., "Benjamin Hawkins' Trip through Alabama in 1796," *Ala. Hist. Quar.*, Vol. XXXI, 1969

Historic Homes of Alabama, Nat'l League of Amer. Penwomen, Birmingham, Ala., 1935

Indians in Alabama, edited by Marie Bankhead Owen, *Ala. Hist. Quar.*, Vol 12, 1950

Jemison, Grace, Historic Tales of Talladega, Paragon Press Montgomery, 1959

Jordan, Weymouth T., *Hugh Davis and His Alabama Plantation*, U. of Ala. Press, 1948

Kelley, Welibourn, *Alabama Empire*, Rinehart, N.W., 1957

Kinnaird, Lawrence, "International Rivalry in the Creek Country," *Fla. Hist. Quar.* Vol. 10, Oct. 1931

Milfort, Gen. LeClerc, *Memoir of Travels in the Creek Nation*, R.R. Donnelly, Chicago, 1956

Mobile Co. Records, Book 19, part 2, p. 231, Weatherford

Moore, Albert B., *History of Alabama*, U. of Ala. Press, 1927

Neeley, Mary Ann Ogleby, "Lachlan McGillivray, A Scot on the Alabama Frontier," *Ala. Hist. Quar.*, Vol. XXXVI, Spring, 1974

Owen, Thomas M., *History, of Alabama*, Vol III, S.J. Clarke, Chicago, 1921

____, *Story of Alabama*, Vol V, N.Y., 1949

Parker, Prescott A., *Story of the Tensaw*, Montrose, Ala., 1922

Pickett, A. J., *History of Alabama*, 1962 reprint

Riley, B.F., *Makers and Romance of Alabama History*, Montgomery, Ala., 1948 reprint

Ritter, Ed, "Horrible Ft. Mims Massacre," *Ala. Journal*, Jan. 20, 1947, dateline Fairhope, Ala.

Royal, Anne Newport, *Letters from Alabama: 1817-1822*, U. of Ala. Press 1969

Tarvin, Dr. Marion E., The Muscogee or Creek Indians, *Ala. Hist. Quar.*, Fall, 1955, written 1939, Galveston, Texas

"Tate, David, *Alabama Historical Quarterly*, Vol. XIX, "Letters to David Moniac"

Tatum, Major Howell, "First Survey of Alabama River, August 1914," *Ala. Hist. Quar.*, Vol II, Topo notes

"Weatherford, William," *Dict. of Amer. Biog.*, Vol. 19, NN., 1936

Woodward, Thomas S., Reminiscences of Creek or Muskogee Indians, Weatherford Printing Press, Tuscaloosa, Ala., 1939

About the Author

Helen Friedman Blackshear served from 1995 to 1999 as Alabama's eighth poet laureate. A native and present resident of Tuscaloosa, she lived in Montgomery from 1934 to 2003. She has three daughters, eight grandchildren, and fourteen great-grandchildren. A graduate of Agnes Scott College, she also has an M.A. from the University of Alabama. She is the author of *Mother Was a Rebel, Southern Smortgasbord, Creek Captives, Alabama Album, Silver Songs* and *From Peddlar to Philanthropist: The Friedmn Story*. She also edited *These I Would Keep*, an anthology of poems by Alabama's first through ninth poet laureates. She has served as treasurer and vice-presiden of the Alabama Poetry Society and as president of the Alabama Writers' Conclave. She was Poet of the Year in 1986 and received the Distinguished Service Award from the Conclave in 1987.

www.ingramcontent.com/pod-product-compliance
Lightning Source LLC
Chambersburg PA
CBHW020005050426
42450CB00005B/321